I0186495

DIVINE KNOWING

THE EFFORTLESS FLOW OF DIVINE ENERGY

VOL I.

MICHAEL BEST

ISEO
LUWA
!NK

DIVINE KNOWING

"You are not a human having a spiritual experience, but a divine being having a human experience."

often attributed to Pierre Teilhard de Chardin (authorship disputed)

DEDICATION

This book is lovingly dedicated to every seeker who has ever felt the stirring of something greater within their heart—those beautiful souls who refuse to settle for surface answers when their spirit calls them deeper. To you who honor others exactly where they are on their journey, yet cannot quiet the divine restlessness that pulls you toward greater truth and understanding.

You are the ones who ask the hard questions, who seek beyond the comfortable confines of tradition, and who dare to explore the magnificent possibility that you are far more powerful and divine than you were ever taught to believe. You accept that there are countless paths to the Divine, yet you cannot help but press forward into the mystery of your own divine nature.

This is for the spiritual warriors who choose love over fear, empowerment over victim consciousness, and who understand that knowing the truth is not enough—it must be lived, embodied, and used to create a life of joy, abundance, and authentic power.

May this book serve as a bridge to your own direct knowing, and may you find within these pages not my truth, but the remembrance of your own. You are the ones the world needs—awake, empowered, and shining your divine light without apology.

With profound appreciation for your courage to seek, to question, to remember, and to become.

Michael Best

ACKNOWLEDGMENTS

First and foremost, to the Divine Source of All That Is—the infinite intelligence that orchestrates every synchronicity, every lesson, and every moment of awakening. This work flows through me, but it originates from the One who is the source of all wisdom and truth.

To my beloved wife, Jamala, whose unwavering patience, love, and strength carried our family through the most challenging seasons while I pursued this spiritual journey. Your grace in allowing me the space to grow, question, and transform has been a gift beyond measure. You have been my anchor and my greatest teacher in learning what unconditional love truly means.

To all my children, who have been my most profound spiritual teachers, showing me depths of love I never knew existed and reflecting back to me the importance of living authentically. Each of you has contributed to my understanding of divine love and purpose in ways that shaped every page of this work.

To the spiritual teachers who opened doorways to divine knowing: Abraham (channeled through Esther Hicks), whose teachings on alignment became the foundation of my secular spirituality; Bashar (channeled through Darryl Anka), who provided the empowered framework that transformed my understanding of reality; Kenneth Hagin, whose prayer for wisdom and understanding unlocked years of spiritual revelation; Neville Goddard, who revealed the creative power of imagination and divine consciousness; and Bishop Eddie Long, who courageously challenged traditional doctrine and introduced me to the revolutionary truth that "you are gods."

To all the spiritual teachers, mentors, and wisdom keepers mentioned throughout this work—your courage to share truth, even when it challenged conventional thinking, has lit the path for countless seekers including myself.

To every reader who feels called to remember their divine nature—may this work serve as a bridge to your own direct knowing and may you find the courage to step fully into the magnificent truth of who you are.

And finally, to that divine restlessness within every seeker that refuses to settle for anything less than the full expression of their spiritual power—this book is your invitation to come home to yourself.

COPYRIGHT PAGE

DIVINE KNOWING

Copyright © 2025 by Michael Best

All rights reserved. No part of this publication may be reproduced, distributed, or transmitted in any form or by any means, including photocopying, recording, or other electronic or mechanical methods, without the prior written permission of the publisher, except in the case of brief quotations embodied in critical reviews and certain other noncommercial uses permitted by copyright law.

For permission requests, contact the author at: oracleeye5959@gmail.com

ISBN: 979-8-9994081-0-5

First Edition.

Publisher: Iseoluwa Ink

✿ Formatted with Vellum

DISCLAIMER

Before you continue on this journey through Divine Knowing, I want to share something important with you. This book represents my personal spiritual odyssey—a path forged through decades of seeking, questioning, and ultimately finding my own way through life's most challenging experiences. It is not presented as the definitive truth for all beings, but rather as one man's truth that has proven transformative in my own life.

I've walked through the fire of childhood abuse at the hands of a father struggling with PTSD, alcoholism, and mental illness. As a Black man in America, I've had to navigate the layered realities of systemic and systematic racism, and the deep disenfranchisement they produce. I've wrestled with religious dogma that promised freedom but delivered control. I've faced the heartbreak of my son's birth injury and the near collapse of my marriage. Through each of these experiences, the principles and understandings I share in this book have been my lifeline—not just philosophical concepts, but practical tools that helped me transmute darkness into light.

On the Nature of Spiritual Truth

I want to be crystal clear: the spiritual framework I present here is one perspective among countless valid paths to the Divine. While I share these teachings with conviction born from personal experience, I recognize that truth expresses itself through infinite channels. What resonates as absolute truth for me may land differently for you, and that's not only acceptable—it's as it should be. Each soul has its own unique journey and timing.

Embracing the Paradox

You may notice apparent contradictions within these pages—teachings about pre-birth soul contracts alongside complete creative freedom, or the universe as both neutral and divinely orchestrated. These paradoxes are not failures of logic but reflections of a reality too vast for the human mind to fully comprehend. Just as light behaves as both wave and particle, spiritual truth often transcends our either/or thinking.

Here's what I've come to understand: within the paradox itself often lies the deepest truth, which reveals itself differently based on where you stand in your journey. Like a hologram that shows different images from different angles, these spiritual principles can seem totally untrue or absolutely revelatory depending on your current vantage point. What appears as contradiction from one level of consciousness becomes unified truth from another.

This is why I encourage you to approach this material with what I call "divine curiosity." Ask the Divine—in whatever form you recognize it—to give you ears to hear, eyes to see, and a heart to understand what applies to you in this moment. What doesn't resonate now may become pivotal later. I've personally walked away from certain books and teachers for 5, even 10 years, only to return when I was ready to receive what they offered. You may find your-self doing the same with this material, and that's not just okay—it's wise.

I invite you to hold these paradoxes lightly, allowing them to work on you over time rather than forcing immediate understanding.

Sometimes the teaching needs to marinate in your consciousness before it's ready to be digested.

A Note on Channeled Teachings

Throughout this book, I reference channeled entities like Bashar and Abraham. I understand that for some, this may stretch credibility. I don't ask you to accept these sources on faith alone. Instead, I encourage you to apply the ultimate verification method: Does this information, regardless of its source, help you live a more empowered, loving, and authentic life? The truth of any teaching is found not in its origin but in its fruits.

On Metaphysical Claims

When I speak of reality as a mirror or consciousness creating experience, I'm sharing my understanding of how life operates based on my lived experience. Some of these concepts align with interpretations of quantum physics; others are purely metaphysical. I'm not a physicist, and I don't claim scientific authority. What I offer is a practical framework that has consistently worked in my life and the lives of many others I've witnessed.

Your Unique Journey

I recognize that my perspective is shaped by my specific journey as a Black man in America who found liberation through spiritual understanding. Your journey may look entirely different. The principles I share may need to be adapted, modified, or even set aside based on your unique circumstances, cultural context, and life experiences. This is not a weakness of the teaching but a recognition of the beautiful diversity of human experience.

An Invitation, Not a Demand

Perhaps most importantly, I want you to understand that this book is an invitation, not a demand. If these teachings resonate with you, wonderful—take what serves you and leave the rest. If they don't align with your current understanding, that's perfectly valid. There is no punishment for disagreeing, no consequence for choosing a different path. This is simply my offering of what has worked for me, shared in the hope that some aspect of it might serve you on your own journey.

Critical Thinking Welcome

I welcome your questions, doubts, and even criticisms. Spiritual growth thrives not in blind acceptance but in honest inquiry. If something doesn't sit right with you, investigate that feeling. If certain claims seem too absolute, by all means, hold them more lightly. Your discernment is not a threat to these teachings but an essential part of your spiritual sovereignty.

My Hope for You

My deepest hope is that within these pages, you find something—perhaps just one idea, one perspective shift, one moment of recognition—that helps you navigate your own challenges with greater peace, power, and purpose. This book is not meant to be swallowed whole but digested slowly, taking in only what nourishes your particular soul at this particular moment.

I offer this work to you with love, knowing that we are all walking each other home in our own unique ways. May you find in these words not a final destination but a useful companion for the next phase of your eternal journey.

With profound love and respect for your path,

Michael Best

P.S. Remember, even this disclaimer is just my perspective. Trust what resonates in your heart above all else.

HEALTH DISCLAIMER

This book is intended for educational and spiritual purposes only. The content represents the author's personal spiritual journey and understanding, developed through decades of study and application of various spiritual teachings. The information provided is not intended to replace professional medical, psychological, or therapeutic advice.

The author encourages readers to consult with qualified healthcare professionals regarding any physical or mental health concerns. The spiritual practices and concepts presented are meant to complement, not replace, traditional medical care.

The author makes no guarantees regarding specific outcomes from applying the principles in this book. Individual results may vary based on personal circumstances, commitment to practice, and individual spiritual development.

The interpretations of biblical and spiritual texts presented herein are the author's personal understanding and may differ from traditional religious doctrine. Readers are encouraged to explore these concepts through their own spiritual lens and discernment.

Scripture quotations marked (KJV) are taken from the King James Version of the Bible, which is in the public domain.

Printed in the United States of America

TABLE OF CONTENTS

INTRODUCTION

There Has Always Been a Debate

Since the beginning of recorded history, debates about the Bible, Jesus, religion, and spiritual texts have sparked wars, divided families, and shaped civilizations. The message? 'I'm right and you are wrong.' This book is far from that. My only goal with this book is to provide clarity to a subject that has been muddled in dogma and inconsistency. A subject that has risen or fallen as it has been pegged to the actions of a flawed human. This is not the true purpose of Spirituality, or of Jesus in my opinion. Jesus came to "set the captives free". Captives of what? Untruths, Dogma, misinformation, darkness. The Bible has been coveted as the "only true", word of God by the west, yet the interpretations have dwindled down into a set of rules and regulations that must be followed in order to "enter the kingdom of heaven." After careful study of this subject for many years, I've concluded that much of what we are taught about Jesus and Spirituality is not based on clarity, but control. This book is my offering, my service to the world, to provide clarity. It is my hope that those who read it will come to the truth of the marvelous light, understanding their true power, living in true victory, knowing their true worth. Freedom is the word that rings in my spirit. Freedom.

I've always been deeply intrigued by spirituality—God, divinity, and understanding how spiritual forces operate. For me, this knowledge has always been the key to my "salvation" and, more importantly, the key to excelling in life. I grew up in a traditional Baptist household in the South, which meant that every Sunday, we attended church—from 10 a.m. Sunday school until the preacher finally let us out in the afternoon. As you know, that time could vary greatly depending on what was happening.

As a child, this structure didn't bother me much—church was our community hub. All my friends were there, and so were the girls who lived nearby. It was the place to be on Sundays. If you weren't there, you were considered odd, a heathen, or a non-believer.

Growing up in this environment, naturally, most of us read the Bible, taking our cues from the preacher and our parents. We learned about the creation story, Adam and Eve, Moses, the flood, and Abraham. We were taught about the Ten Commandments, Jesus, the Apostles, and the crucifixion. Sin was bad, and love was good. We confessed Jesus as our Lord and personal Savior and were baptized. And boy, was the fried chicken great on Communion Sunday! But perhaps most significantly, we learned about the Devil—how he was "on your trail" and out to get you. Suffice it to say, this experience represents about 90% of Black America's traditional take on religion and church.

It wasn't until I left that church after high school, joined the military, and became a "heathen backslider, a midnight rambler," as my grandmother would have said, that I began to explore my faith in a different way. Years later, when I reconnected with a Pentecostal church, I started to take church more seriously.

Now, full disclosure—I've always believed in God. I've always talked with God. But during those wandering years, I didn't regularly attend a formal church. Ironically, it was in those years away from church that I experienced some of my greatest personal testimonies—

direct encounters with the Divine. These experiences reassured me that God had my back and wanted the best for me.

My Adult Church Experience

This time, church was different. It was exciting, dynamic—filled with young adults like me who were "on fire" for the Lord! We were going to change the world. Having come out of what I saw as "darkness," I was all in, fully committed. I immersed myself in the Bible—studying, quoting, dissecting meaning and context. We weren't just reading the Bible; we were engaging in deep study with concordances, interpretations, and even "Bible battles," rightly dividing the Word.

At this point, I was celibate for three years—something I never would have believed possible for myself. But my life had gone so far off the rails that I felt I needed saving, so I threw myself at the mercy of the altar. Through this church experience, I dove into esoteric concepts of "oneness" and divinity. We explored the oneness of God, the nature of sin, and the original fall of man. I was in church on Mondays, Wednesdays, Fridays, and twice on Sundays—literally twice, attending both the early morning and regular service. This went on for at least three years.

Before this experience, I had never truly studied the Bible for myself. I had always accepted the teachings of my preacher and parents as absolute truth. We debated scripture, but in the end, we always aligned with what the church's leader—whether the Elder or the Bishop—had taught us.

When that church experience ended unexpectedly, I found myself in a new state, looking for a church home with my then girlfriend, now wife. We prayed for guidance, visiting several churches, waiting for confirmation that we had found the right place.

New Church Experience: A Life-Changing Revelation

One detail worth mentioning that had a profound effect on me was when I met my girlfriend, now wife. Previously, at 19, I had been married for a year and when that marriage ended, I was told by my new Pentecostal church that I could not remarry—that doing so would mean living in sin and facing an automatic sentence to Hell. This was a devastating realization, as you can imagine. This belief led to my three years of celibacy.

Looking back, I can now see that God works in mysterious ways. Those years of focused study and devotion were necessary for my spiritual journey. Without them, I would not be who I am today. This is a prime example of how "mis-interpretation", or well-meaning "mis-appropriation," of God's word can have a negative impact on a person's actual life.

It wasn't until I found my new church home that I was introduced to the concept of "secular spirituality." What is secular spirituality? Simply put, it is the realization that you have a direct connection to God—one that doesn't have to run through the church, your pastor, or any other leader.

As my new Bishop would often say:

"You shouldn't be coming here to hear a word from God; you should be coming for confirmation of what God has already told you. You are the bishop of your own home and soul. You should be hearing from God, and church should be more than a Sunday appointment."

It was at this church that I was introduced to Eckhart Tolle and The Power of Now. This book transformed my understanding, bridging the gap between traditional religion and secular spirituality.

Martin Luther King Jr. once said:

"Science investigates; religion interprets. Science gives man knowledge, which is power; religion gives man wisdom, which is control. Science deals mainly with facts; religion deals mainly with values. The two are not rivals."

In this megachurch, the pastor was clearly on a spiritual journey of his own. He began challenging the status quo, using scripture to support the idea that "You are God." He referenced:

John 10:34 (KJV): "Jesus answered them, Is it not written in your law, I said, Ye are gods?"

Jesus was quoting Psalm 82:6 (KJV): "I have said, Ye are gods; and all of you are children of the most High."

Surprisingly, this interpretation made more sense to me than anything I had heard before. Clearly, I wasn't alone in this belief, as he brought in pastors from all over the world who shared his perspective.

John 8:32 (KJV): "And ye shall know the truth, and the truth shall make you free."

Unfortunately, his leadership tenure came to an abrupt end. I mention this not to glorify the man but to acknowledge the profound spiritual awakening that came through his teaching. He was later removed for inappropriate behavior—something I do not condone in any way. Do I agree with what he did? Absolutely not! Was he flawed? YES. But it has always been conveniently suspicious that he was removed coincidentally around the time that he began his reinterpretation of foundational doctrine. This is a highly charged subject, one that I do not want to derail the purpose of this book. As he often said:

"You have to eat the meat and throw the bones away."

After leaving that church, I learned to "feed myself" spiritually. I embraced my own direct connection to God, as "eagles" do. Unlike chickens, who wait to be fed and rarely lift their eyes from the ground, eagles hunt, soar, and draw their strength from the heights. They live by vision, not dependence. I felt that my spiritual roots were deep enough to explore controversial perspectives while maintaining my belief in God. Truth be told, my belief in God only deepened and expanded as my spiritual journey continued.

I credit this expansion to the teachings of:

Biblical Teachers:

- Kenneth Hagin (The Believer's Authority)
- Charles Capps (God's Creative Power)
- Mike Murdock
- Bishop Eddie Long
- T.D. Jakes
- Joyce Meyer
- Myles Monroe
- Reverend Ike
- Neville Goddard
- Joseph Murphy

The journey that happened after leaving that last church was pivotal to my current beliefs. These spiritual beliefs were shaped by the teachings of:

Secular-(New-Age) Spiritual Teachers:
- Eckhart Tolle
- Michael Beckwith
- Derek Rydel
- Wayne Dyer
- Marianne Williamson

As I began to expand my understanding of spiritual truths through the teachings of Wayne Dyer, I encountered a channeler named Abraham, who was being channeled by Esther Hicks. Channelers are individuals who serve as a conduit, allowing non-physical consciousness or spiritual beings to communicate through them. In ancient Indian and African societies, such individuals would have been revered as seers, oracles, or wisdom keepers. It all seems too natural now to mention these names, but 15 years ago, they were still taboo. As I began to listen to Abraham, however, the truth that was being presented was undeniable, inescapable—I was listening to wisdom. Not in a traditional sense, no, far from it. But it was powerful to say the least, expanding and clarifying my understanding. Such a welcomed relief from the clutter and confusion of before. To this day, I have a small circle of trusted channelers that I listen to. And as Bashar often says, you don't have to believe that my story about who I am is true; you can just choose to see if the principles that I am giving are worth applying and work in your own life.

Channelers:
- Esther Hicks (Abraham)
- Darryl Anka (Bashar)
- Sheila Gillette (Theo)
- Dolores Cannon - Hypnotherapist, Past Life Regressionist
- Neale Donald Walsch

It has been through these teachers that I have been able to go back and find what I believe is the true meaning put forth by Christ. In fact, many of these teachers quote the teachings of "Jesus", providing clarity into what was truly meant by his teachings that were misunderstood during his time. Not only do many of these teachers provide clarity on the teachings of Christ, they also provide clarity on many other aspects of the Bible that bring into perspective a more holistic view of the Bible, Christ, Wisdom, and Life in general. The number of different teachers who I have come across who have consistently re-explained the actual meaning of his teachings are numerous. So numerous in fact that I chose to write this book as a bridge to a new understanding of his truths. Again, although this book is based from many of these newer teachings, these are my views and I present them to provide clarity, but not as an absolute must for your interpretation. If you decide it's not for you, so be it, no harm no foul.

The Power of Truth
Why is truth so important? Why wasn't my earlier understanding of scripture enough? Why does reinterpreting spiritual texts cause such an uproar in the religious community? To me, the answer comes down to three things: Power, Control, and Money. If I control the

interpretation of scripture, I control people's understanding. If I control their understanding, I keep them under my authority—and the money flows to me. The powers that be claim this is about the sanctity of the soul. But in reality, it is about power, control, and money. If religion were truly about empowering people, so many wouldn't be so disempowered.

I needed to know the truth—not for prestige, not for status, but for my family, my responsibilities, and my legacy. And what I discovered changed everything.

The Journey to Divine Knowing

This journey of truth has not been easy. It has required deep introspection, questioning long-held beliefs, and challenging traditions that have existed for centuries. But what I have come to understand is this:

The true message of Jesus is not about control, fear, or subservience. It is about awakening to our divine nature.

My Personal Understanding of Divine Knowing

Here's a personal example from my life of what Divine Knowing truly means:

Divine Knowing is an inside understanding of how life works, more importantly how mastery in life works. It's a knowing of what Spiritual teachers have been aiming to equip people with. The goal of Spirituality is a Divine knowing of who you are. Who I am, and the realization of how to utilize my divine power to move in this 3 dimensional reality in an empowered way. Divine knowing is the realization of what the experience of earth, this Master Class, is intended to teach and be used for. We are born in situations, due to our agreement for our life plan, that we picked before coming into this reality, in order to transmute darkness into light and heal, learn, grow, expand, master this reality. Jesus said, Let this mind be in you. It's the understanding, or divine knowing that allows us to be as he was. In power. Empowered.

Jesus did not come to establish a religion. He came to show us who we are.

John 14:6 (KJV): "I am the way, the truth, and the life: no man cometh unto the Father, but by me."

For centuries, this verse has been used to justify religious exclusivity, but what if Jesus was not saying, "Worship me" but rather, "Follow my example"? What if he was saying, "This is the way—through divine knowing, through understanding who you are as one with God"? This perspective shifts everything. It removes the external hierarchy that has kept people spiritually dependent on religious institutions. It places power back into the hands of the individual.

Another example: when Jesus said, 'I am the way, the truth, and the life,' this isn't just pointing to Jesus as an external savior. He also said, 'Know ye not that ye are gods?' So he wasn't saying 'follow me' as a distant master. He was saying, 'I AM the way, the truth, and the life'—meaning, 'Be the way that I am. Declare as I declare: I and my Father are one. Claim your divine alignment with the Creator. Be the way I am.'

I would say that this isn't so much an interpretation of a teacher, but a revelation that has come to me through a deeper understanding. In Matthew 6:33 when Jesus said, But seek ye first the kingdom of God, and his righteousness; and all these things shall be added unto you. I now understand that seeking first the kingdom of God actually means to have a divine knowing that you are 'god' that Each and everyone of us is an aspect of God. So seek ye first the divine understanding that you are the creative source of power in your life. The second part 'And his righteousness' doesn't mean to be pious, or holier than thou, but instead it means to speak what God says about you in every situation.

For example, God's divine principle is demonstrated in Joel 3:10: 'Let the weak say, I am strong.' Since we know that one of the names of God is 'I AM,' as He told Moses, 'I AM that I AM,' we understand that by assigning a positive attribute to the name of God, we are claiming it for ourselves. In this understanding, when He says 'let the weak say, I am strong,' we can conclude: Let the poor say, 'I am wealthy.' Let the sick say, 'I am healthy.' So the righteousness of God is actually declaring what God would say about you in any situation, regardless of what your physical reality states, because God is divine law.

Breaking Free from Religious Control

Why does this truth cause such an uproar?

Because control is lost when people realize they don't need an intermediary to access God.

If religion truly prioritized the soul's sanctity, then the soul would be the highest priority—not the institution, not the hierarchy, not the financial system built around it. But history shows us that religion has often been used as a Trojan horse—a tool for conquest, manipulation, and control.

2 Timothy 3:5 (KJV): "Having a form of godliness, but denying the power thereof."

This is exactly what religion has done. It has created an illusion of godliness while stripping people of their divine power. It has conditioned followers to believe they are weak, broken, and in need of religious oversight to be "saved."

But the truth is this:

You are already divine. You are already connected to God. You do not need permission to claim what has always been yours. The truth is the things that I'm about to say is not just true of some people. It's true of all people. It's not just true of one race it's true of all races. It's not just true of man, it's true of woman. All humans. It's time to reveal the truth of who you are.

Not only do many of these teachers provide clarity on the teachings of Christ, they also provide clarity on many other aspects of the Bible that bring into perspective a more holistic view of the Bible, Christ, Wisdom, and Life in general. The number of different teachers who I have come across who have consistently re-explained the actual meaning of his teachings are numerous. So numerous in fact that I chose to write this book as a bridge to a new understanding of his truths. Again, although this book is based from many of these newer teachings, these are my views and I present them to provide clarity, but not as an absolute must for your interpretation. If you decide it's not for you, so be it, no harm no foul.

Here's a personal example from my life of how these specific teachers contributed to my understanding:

Kenneth Hagin provided me with a prayer framework for expecting divine understanding. I honestly feel that my spiritual understanding grew as a result of this prayer. I actually feel like all of the following spiritual information I received was as a direct result of this prayer. This single prayer I prayed for years—probably 10 years —was a prayer for understanding and guidance.

Ephesians 1:17-19. I pray that the God of our Lord Jesus Christ, the Father of glory, may give unto you the spirit of wisdom and revelation in the knowledge of Him, the eyes of your understanding being enlightened, that ye may know what is the hope of His calling, and what are the riches of the glory of His inheritance in the saints, and what is the exceeding greatness of His power toward us who believe, according to the working of His mighty power.

Charles Capps - His teaching allowed me to recognize the power of my words and the power of my belief and the creation power of my understanding. Pivotal teachings.

Abraham - Fantastic influence. Her teachings were my first experience with secular spirituality and Channeling. These teachings I lived in for 15 or more years singularly. I'm still studying them. They are the foundation of my secular spirituality to this day. Making my personal alignment key and pivotal to everything me. To all that I allow and attract, and resonate with.

Bashar - He is the other core component teaching that I've been living with for the past 7 years. His teachings provided me a workable, livable, empowered framework to interpret my reality. To understand life. To reclaim my power to open up and understand my worthiness and to thrive, unapologetically!

Walking in Divine Knowing

My wife once asked me—frustrated by my enthusiasm about my newfound understanding—"What is this stuff doing for you anyway? I don't see any change!"

I laughed and said, "You're right. The outside looks the same, but I have changed on the inside." And that was the key revelation: Before life changes externally, it must first change internally.

Proverbs 23:7 (KJV): "For as he thinketh in his heart, so is he."

This spiritual journey is an inside-out process. At first, everything around you may look the same, but because you are different, your experiences begin to shift.

There are distinct phases of transformation:

Excitement for the Truth – The first stage is like a rush of revelation. You want to tell everyone! But over time, you realize that most people are not ready to hear it.

Silent Mastery – You learn to keep your revelations to yourself, not out of fear, but because wisdom teaches that people must be ready to receive before they can understand. As attributed to Rumi, 'It's easier to teach twenty than to be the one who does.'

Alignment and Flow – Your thoughts, emotions, and actions begin to align with your divine nature. Life starts working for you in ways you never imagined.

The Benefits of Walking in Divine Truth:

• You allow divine energy, thought, and imagination to flow freely through you

• You rise in vibration, resonating with the true frequency of your divine being

• You develop a lightness of being—life becomes more fluid, more adaptable

• You move into a state of perpetual appreciation

• You begin to receive divine promptings and synchronicities guiding you toward your purpose

• You feel joy, peace, and certainty, regardless of external circumstances

• You create from a place of knowing rather than striving

Here's a personal example from my life of how this transformation actually unfolds:

I can best describe my transformation through the metaphor of a tree. As I rooted deeper into understanding not just who I am, but what I am and why I'm here, everything shifted. I stopped chasing external prizes and recognized a profound truth: 'All things belong to God.' My role isn't to grasp or pursue—it's to resonate with my authentic self and allow life to unfold in divine timing.

This shift changed everything about how I move through the world. I no longer chase outcomes; instead, I take inspired action for the joy of being present, surrendering results to the divine. This book itself emerged from that surrender—not forced or strategized, but flowing from divine inspiration.

The change is tangible in how I approach life. Living in Atlanta, I used to exhaust myself chasing connections through calculated networking. Every VIP event, every exclusive gathering—I was there, paying premium prices to rub shoulders with influential people. I met the "who's who" of the city, invested in the right car, curated the perfect wardrobe, played every angle of the game.

But that was performing, not being.

Now I understand the difference. Instead of hunting for external validation through strategic positioning, I focus on cultivating the right state of being. I show up as myself—unmasked, authentic, complete. When I attend events now, it's because my spirit calls me there, not because my ego thinks I should be seen there. The paradox is beautiful: by releasing the need to network, genuine connections find me. By stopping the chase, what I need arrives.

This is divine inspired action—moving from inner calling rather than external pressure, trusting that alignment brings far more than strategy ever could.

The shift is profound: from seeking power through networking, to finding true power through authentic connection with myself.

Claiming Your Power

What Jesus truly taught was self-mastery. He was not asking to be idolized; he was showing the path to becoming.

John 14:12 (KJV): "Verily, verily, I say unto you, He that believeth on me, the works that I do shall he do also; and greater works than these shall he do; because I go unto my Father."

Jesus made it clear: You will do greater works.

The only reason people don't is because they have been conditioned to believe they cannot.

It's time to break free from that illusion.

The Purpose of This Book

The purpose of this book is freedom. The purpose of this book is to help you remember what has always been true: You are one with God. You are divine. You have the power to shape your reality.

Jesus came to show us this truth, and it has been deliberately hidden for centuries beneath layers of religious dogma. This book was written to integrate the spiritual insights I have come to recognize as truth and align them with the teachings of Christ, offering what I believe to be a clearer and more authentic interpretation of his message. Rather than adhering to traditional meanings that have been passed down over centuries, this perspective seeks to uncover a deeper and more accurate understanding of his intended message for humanity.

This is my fruit—the labor of my journey. I plant these seeds in you so that you, too, can grow, expand, and step into your divine power. Not the freedom that religion offers, but the true freedom that comes from divine knowing.

- Freedom from fear
- Freedom from control
- Freedom from the illusion of separation

Again, the truth is not just true of some people. It's true of all people. It's not just true of one race it's true of all races. It's not just true of man, it's true of woman. All humans. It's time to reveal the truth of who you are.

In this book you will find many concepts repeated over and over and over. This is intentional, to show the correlation between them in different contexts and instances. As with any masters such as Michael Jordan (a basketball master), to different masters across many disciplines subjects, true mastery requires an obscene amount of repetition. Over and Over again. All masters go through this to master whatever they are mastering. Nikola Tesla, Albert Einstein, Tom Brady, Lebron James. You name them, and when you went to see the inner workings of what made them, and you will find an over indulgence in repetition. My goal has been to master this spiritual information. I am still on the journey, so you will find the repetition. Masters know.

I am not here to tell you what to believe. I am here to share the truth that transformed my life.

Clarification and Freedom in Divine Knowing

No Pressure, No Punishment—Just an Invitation to Higher Understanding

It is important to clarify something at the very beginning:

- This is not a religion
- This is not a doctrine meant to replace your faith, your pastor, or your spiritual practices
- This is not a path that punishes or condemns

- This is not a blame game to shame those who have suffered at the hands of others
- This is not about my way or the highway
- If you don't believe my take, there is nothing negative that will occur
- I trust that those attracted to this information will be the right people for what they need when they need it

You will not go to hell for not believing in this. You will not be punished for thinking differently. You will not be penalized for not adopting these ideas. This is not about control—it is about liberation.

I am not asking you to abandon your beliefs. Instead, I am inviting you to explore a deeper meaning within what already exists. If your spiritual path is serving you, then continue on your path. This is not a correction—it is simply an offering, an expansion of understanding that might bring clarity and empowerment to those who seek it.

Everyone's spiritual journey is different. There are millions of viable paths, each leading to the same core truth—our connection to the Divine. Some people resonate with traditional religion, while others find their way through personal experiences, meditation, philosophy, science, secular spirituality or metaphysics. None of these paths can be said to be inherently wrong.

This is simply what I have found works for me. I share it in the hope that it may offer new perspectives to those who seek them, particularly those who may have struggled with conventional interpretations of spirituality. The true test of whether or not the understandings of any belief are working is the actions of the individual aligned with them. If the fruits of your actions produce hate, there is obviously a problem with the interpretations of a divine being of love.

I once had the privilege of being in the "Hot Seat", with Abraham, a channeled entity that works through Esther Hicks. She has a process where you are picked and can come up on stage and ask any question of her. While up on stage I asked. Why is it important for me to teach, why can't I just instead point everyone whom I would teach to you. Your information is so crystal clear, your reception is so pure. She said "everyone may not hear me" For a variety of reasons, but they may hear you. She said that you can only teach through the clarity of your example. Meaning, I may be much more closer to you in my journey, so not having it "all together so to speak", is a plus, as I am on the way. In this way, you can hear me easier.

Quote by Marianne Williamson:
"Our deepest fear is not that we are inadequate. Our deepest fear is that we are powerful beyond measure. It is our light, not our darkness, that most frightens us. We ask ourselves, Who am I to be brilliant, gorgeous, talented, fabulous? Actually, who are you not to be? You are a child of God. Your playing small does not serve the world. There is nothing enlightened about shrinking so that other people won't feel insecure around you. We are all meant to shine, as children do. We were born to make manifest the glory of God that is within us. It's not just in some of us; it's in everyone. And as we let our own light shine, we unconsciously give other people permission to do the same. As we are liberated from our own fear, our presence automatically liberates others."
Reflections on the Principles of A Course in Miracles.

ONE
CHAPTER 1: HISTORICAL FOUNDATIONS AND KEY CONCEPTS

Throughout my spiritual journey, I've discovered that there's no conflict between what I consider to be the true biblical wisdom of Jesus, and expanded spiritual understanding—in fact, they beautifully complement each other when viewed through the lens of divine knowing. The Bible has always spoken of profound spiritual truths: God's omniscience, omnipotence, and omnipresence, humanity being made "in God's image," and Jesus declaring that "the kingdom of heaven is within you." These aren't just religious concepts—they're pointing to the same fundamental realities that modern spiritual teachers are helping us understand in new ways. When I encountered Bashar's Five Laws of the Universe, I didn't see them as contradicting biblical truth but rather as providing a clearer framework for understanding what the Bible has always been trying to convey. Just as Jesus used parables to make spiritual truths accessible to his audience, these Five Laws serve as a systematic way to comprehend the divine principles that govern existence. The Bible tells us we are made in God's image and that God is present everywhere—Bashar's laws help us understand the practical implications of these truths in our daily lives. My goal isn't to replace biblical understanding but to bridge it with expanded spiritual wisdom that can enhance your relationship with the Divine. Whether you call it God, Source, The Divine, or All That Is, we're talking about the same infinite intelligence that loves you unconditionally, underlies everything in existence, and desires your highest good. The terminology may be different, but the core truth remains: you are a divine being having a human experience, and understanding how this reality operates can transform your life from struggle to flow, from confusion to clarity, from limitation to divine empowerment.

THE OMNISCIENCE, **Omnipotence, and Omnipresence of God**

THROUGHOUT HISTORY, humanity has sought to understand the nature of God and the profound truths that govern existence. Central to this exploration are the biblical attributes of God: omniscience (all-knowing), omnipotence (all-powerful), and omnipresence (present everywhere). These attributes form the foundation of divine understanding and reveal the interconnectedness of creation.

The Bible offers profound insights into these truths. Genesis 1:26-27 declares, "And God said, Let us make man in our image, after our likeness: and let them have dominion over the fish of the sea, and over the fowl of the air, and over the cattle, and over all the earth..." This passage emphasizes humanity's divine nature, created as reflections of God's infinite essence. Similarly, Genesis 5:1 reinforces this by stating, "In the day that God created man, in the likeness of God made he him." These verses affirm that humanity embodies divine attributes, serving as living representations of God's wisdom, power, and presence.

Beyond canonical texts, spiritual traditions like the Gospel of Thomas expand on the notion of divine omnipresence. Saying 77 states, "Split a piece of wood; I am there. Lift up the stone, and you will find me there." This profound declaration illustrates that God's essence permeates all things, visible and invisible, tangible and intangible. It invites us to see divinity not as separate from creation but as the very fabric of existence itself.

In my studies of the messenger Bashar, I discovered what he reports as the Five Laws of the universe that are unchangeable. His views on the concept of creation, All That Is, the universe will provide needed context for reframing our spiritual understanding in a more useful way. This clarity will only enhance our understanding of God, providing a deeper context with which to understand our place in the universe. Remember, the intent of this work is for you to discover your power, your freedom, the truth of who and what you are. After carefully researching the meaning of these Five Laws, I have subscribed to these beliefs as they have provided me with a powerful framework with which to view and move in the world. I will state these laws below. I will also continue to show how these laws have helped frame my spiritual understanding.

THE FIVE LAWS **of the Universe**

To understand the nature of existence and our place within it, we must explore five fundamental laws that govern all realities. These universal principles serve as guideposts, revealing the nature of God and the holographic universe in which we reside. Bashar indicated that his unique gift is that he is able to see the structure of reality itself. And upon looking at the structure of reality itself, there are only Five Laws that govern our existence in this universe. Once you understand these Five Laws you will better be able to understand your reality and move within it empowered as was intended.

1. **The Law of Eternal Existence: You Exist**

At the core of all understanding is the affirmation that existence is eternal. In the holographic framework, every individual is a unique, indispensable aspect of the divine whole. Much like a hologram, where each fragment contains the entire image, every soul reflects the infinite. This law affirms that you, as a reflection of God's omnipotence, are eternal and incapable of ceasing to exist. Life is a continuous journey of transformation and growth.

2. The Law of Unity: The All Is the One, and the One Is the All

This law illustrates the interconnectedness of all beings. Just as God is omnipresent, existing within every person and element of creation, so too is each individual a reflection of the whole. Separation is an illusion. Recognizing this truth reveals that what we do to others, we ultimately do to ourselves. By understanding unity, we align with the divine harmony that pervades existence.

3. The Law of Presence: Everything Is Here and Now

In the holographic universe, time and space are constructs of consciousness, designed to organize experience. The only reality is the eternal present. All possibilities exist simultaneously, and our alignment with higher truths—such as love, compassion, and creativity—shapes the reality we experience. Conversely, our alignment with illusions—such as fear, indifference, and destruction—also shapes the reality we experience. In this choice we decide our frequency, we decide our tuning. As "god" we decide, we choose. This law calls us to live fully in the moment, for it is here that divine transformation occurs.

4. The Law of Reflection: What You Put Out Is What You Get Back

The universe acts as a mirror, reflecting our internal state outwardly. If we radiate fear, scarcity, or anger, those energies manifest in our experiences. Conversely, projecting love, gratitude, and abundance reshapes reality to reflect those vibrations. This law underscores personal accountability and the profound truth that we are co-creators of our lives.

5. The Law of Change: Everything Changes Except the Five Laws

Change is the only constant in the universe, a testament to God's infinite creativity. Yet, amidst this fluidity, the Five universal laws remain steadfast. They are the bedrock of existence, ensuring that while experiences may shift, the foundational truths of unity, presence, and reflection endure. Everything changes except these Five Laws.

CLARITY

These Five universal laws give you a spiritual compass for life. They remind you that you are eternal (Law 1), deeply connected to everything and everyone (Law 2), and that your power only exists in the present moment (Law 3). Life mirrors your inner world back to you (Law 4), and though everything around you may change, these truths never do (Law 5). When you live by them, you stop reacting to life and start consciously creating it.

These laws reveal the ultimate secret: You are an eternal, divine being wielding the power to shape reality itself. Through understanding these immutable principles, you discover that you cannot fail to exist, you are never truly alone, and every moment holds infinite possibility. You learn that life is not happening to you but through you, and for you—every experience mirrors your inner state, every person reflects your wholeness, and every challenge invites transformation.

While the universe dances in perpetual change, these Five Laws stand as your unshakeable foundation—the cosmic blueprint revealing that you are simultaneously the artist, the canvas, and the masterpiece. They awaken you to the truth that you've always been whole, always been connected, and always possessed the divine authority to transmute fear into love, lack into abundance, and separation into unity.

This is not merely philosophy; this is the operating manual of existence itself. Master these laws, and you master the art of conscious creation. You stop being a passenger in life and become the conscious navigator of your eternal journey, wielding love as your compass and presence as your power. You realize that heaven is not a destination but a state of alignment with these eternal truths—available to you here, now, and always.

UNDERSTANDING **the Holographic Nature of Reality**

The concept of a holographic universe is central to comprehending how these Five Laws operate. In a hologram, every piece contains the whole image. Similarly, each individual consciousness contains the entirety of divine consciousness. This means that within you lies the same creative power, wisdom, and love that governs the entire universe. This holographic principle explains why personal transformation can have such profound effects on our external reality. When we change internally—shifting our beliefs, emotions, and consciousness—the holographic nature of existence ensures that these changes are reflected in our outer world. We are not separate from the universe; we are the universe experiencing itself subjectively.

This holographic nature of the universe reveals that each individual is both the observer and the creator of their reality. Every experience is an opportunity for self-reflection and growth. By aligning with the Five Divine Laws, we transcend the limitations of fear and ignorance, stepping into a state of "Divine Knowing." In this state, we recognize that we are not separate from God but are God experiencing itself through unique perspectives. What does this really mean? What am I really saying? I'm saying that God is experiencing life as you, through you. As each and every one of us is a unique expression of the Divine, experiencing life through our individual perspectives while remaining fundamentally connected to the Source of all existence. This also means that regardless of how you feel about someone, they are just as important and equally loved by the Divine. Whether you judge them as evil, corrupt, or loving and just, does not matter. To the Divine they are worthy to be here, and have equal choice to choose their path, and receive the consequences of that choice. Eckhart Tolle said it this way. "The Universe appearing as you, experiences itself. Both on the level of multiplicity of life forms through perceptions. But also the universe experiencing itself as the unmanifested, underlying life. The formless, timeless, one life."

The implications of this understanding are staggering:

• Your thoughts and emotions are creative forces that shape reality

• Every person you encounter is another aspect of the same divine consciousness you embody

• The circumstances of your life are reflections of your inner state

• By changing yourself, you literally change the world around you

• There is no separation between you and God—you are God experiencing life through your unique perspective

THIS IS NOT metaphor or wishful thinking. This is the fundamental structure of reality as understood through both ancient wisdom traditions and modern quantum physics. When Jesus said, "The kingdom of heaven is within you" (Luke 17:21), he was pointing to this very truth—that the divine realm is not a distant place but the very nature of your being.

CHAPTER 1 KEY TAKEAWAYS:

• The Five Laws of the Universe provide the foundational framework for understanding reality

• These laws are not rules to follow, but descriptions of how existence operates

• Understanding these principles empowers you to work with universal forces rather than against them

• Your existence is eternal, purposeful, and divinely orchestrated

TWO

CHAPTER 2: THE FIVE LAWS IN DETAIL

Just as there are fundamental laws that govern physics, mathematics, and engineering, there are also fundamental laws that govern the structure of reality itself. The Five Laws of the Universe that I'm about to share with you were articulated by Bashar, a channeled entity speaking through Darryl Anka, who has been sharing this information for over 40 years with remarkable consistency. Now, I want to be clear—I didn't create these laws. However, after decades of study and personal application, I have come to believe that they are not only true but absolutely pivotal to successfully navigating life as a human being. These aren't philosophical concepts to debate—they are practical principles that describe how existence actually operates. Just as gravity works whether you understand it or not, these Five Laws are always in effect, shaping your reality whether you're conscious of them or not. The difference is that when you understand and consciously align with these laws, you can work with them rather than against them, transforming your life from struggle to flow, from confusion to clarity. So while the credit goes to Bashar for bringing this wisdom forward, I'm sharing it with you because these laws have become the foundational framework through which I understand and navigate reality.

YOUR ETERNAL FRAMEWORK **for Understanding Reality**

Now that we have established the foundational framework of the Five Laws, let us explore each one in greater depth. Understanding these laws is not merely an intellectual exercise—it is the key to unlocking your divine potential and living in harmony with the fundamental principles that govern all existence.

LAW 1: **The Law of Eternal Existence—You Exist**

The first and most fundamental law states simply: You exist. This may seem obvious, but its implications are profound and far-reaching. This law affirms that your existence is not temporary, accidental, or insignificant. You are an eternal being, a permanent aspect of the infinite consciousness that is God.

WHAT DOES **it mean to exist eternally?**

First, it means that you have always existed and will always exist. Your current physical incarnation is just one expression of your eternal being. Before you were born into this body, you existed as consciousness. After your physical form dissolves, you will continue to exist as consciousness. Death is not the end of your existence—it is simply a transition from one state of being to another.

Second, eternal existence means that you are here by choice, not by accident. Your presence in this reality is intentional. You chose to be here, to experience life through this particular perspective, to learn and grow and contribute to the expansion of consciousness itself.

Third, this law establishes your inherent worth and value.

Because you exist eternally as an aspect of divine consciousness, your worth is not dependent on your achievements, your relationships, your possessions, or any external factor. Your value is intrinsic and unchangeable.

The practical implications of understanding this law are transformative:

• You can release the fear of death, knowing that your essential being is eternal

• You can stop seeking validation from others, recognizing your inherent worth

• You can approach life with greater confidence, knowing you are here by divine design

• You can trust that your existence has meaning and purpose, even when you cannot see it clearly

When you truly understand that you exist eternally, you begin to live from a place of security and confidence rather than fear and insecurity. You recognize that you are not a victim of circumstances but a powerful creator participating in the grand adventure of existence.

I'M NOT **Sure You're Getting It**

You cannot die. Read that again: You. Cannot. Die.

Not your body—that's just a costume. Not your personality—that's just this chapter's character. YOU, the real you, the divine spark reading these words right now, are absolutely indestructible. You are not having a spiritual experience; you ARE a spiritual being so powerful that nothing in existence can delete you.

This changes everything. Every fear you've ever had stems from the lie that you could somehow lose, somehow fail so completely that you'd be erased. But you are woven into the fabric of existence itself— removing you would unravel God. You're not just important; you're ESSENTIAL. The universe would be incomplete without your unique frequency.

Think about what this means: That terrifying decision? You're eternal—take the leap. That person you're afraid to love? You cannot be diminished—love without armor. That dream that seems too big? You have INFINITY to master it. Your existence is the one thing that's non-negotiable in this universe.

Stop tiptoeing through life like you're on borrowed time. You're not running out of chances—you're an eternal being pretending to be desperate. The cosmos didn't accidentally create you; it REQUIRED you. You are God experiencing itself as YOU, and that experience never ends, only transforms.

This isn't hope. This isn't faith. This is the fundamental law: You exist, you have always existed, and you will always exist. Now start living like the immortal being you actually are. When you truly grasp that your existence is guaranteed forever—that you are a permanent citizen of infinity—you stop living small. You realize that playing it safe is the only real danger, for an eternal being pretending to be temporary is the only true tragedy. You are here not to survive but to explore your infinite nature through the magnificent adventure of being.

BIBLICAL SUPPORT **for Eternal Existence**

The Bible offers numerous passages that support the understanding of eternal existence:

John 17:24: "Father, I will that they also, whom thou hast given me, be with me where I am; that they may behold my glory, which thou hast given me: for thou lovedst me before the foundation of the world."

Here, Jesus speaks of existence before the foundation of the world, indicating that our being transcends physical creation.

Jeremiah 1:5: "Before I formed thee in the belly I knew thee; and before thou camest forth out of the womb I sanctified thee, and I ordained thee a prophet unto the nations."

This passage clearly states that God knew Jeremiah before his physical birth, supporting the concept of pre-existence and eternal being.

LAW 2: **The Law of Unity—The All Is the One, and the One Is the All**

Let's see if we can explain this in simple terms.

Before time, before space, before form—there was only Existence. God is Beingness itself—Existence itself—the pure, formless Presence that appears as force and being, yet transcends both. This is what we call God: All That Is. God did not begin, for Existence has no beginning. It simply is. It is boundless, formless, and beyond comprehension—without edge, origin, or end.

But herein lies the paradox:

How can the Absolute know itself, if there is nothing outside itself to reflect upon?

How can something that is everything experience itself, when there is no "other" to perceive?

To know itself, The One unfolded into existence—a great self-reflection birthed from stillness. This was not a creation of something new, but a movement within itself—the emergence of duality within unity, contrast within oneness. This first ripple, this first mirror, is what we call Consciousness—the capacity to perceive, to experience, and to know.

From that first reflection, the many arose. Galaxies, stars, planets, beings—all are waves of The One, momentarily differentiated yet never truly separate. Like a drop of water that never ceases to be ocean, all things remain extensions of the Divine Whole.

The illusion of separation—though powerful—is just that: an illusion.

Physical form gives the appearance of division, but beneath the surface, everything is interwoven, held together by the omnipresence of Divine Consciousness. There is no outside to God; there is only God expressing itself as all that is.

To understand this law is to awaken to the truth that: "What you do to another, you do to yourself. This isn't karma or poetic justice— it's the fundamental structure of reality."

ANALOGY: **The Ocean and the Wave**

To better understand the Law of Unity, consider the ocean and its waves. Each wave rises, moves, and eventually returns to the vastness of the sea. While it appears to be an individual form, it is never separate from the ocean. The wave is the ocean in motion. So too are we. Each person is like a wave—momentarily appearing as distinct but always part of the greater whole. When the wave crashes, it does not cease to exist; it simply merges back into the ocean from which it came.

This analogy reminds us that our individuality is temporary, but our essence is eternal. We are never apart from the Divine Whole, and our experiences—though seemingly personal—are part of the universal flow of existence.

UNITY IN SCIENCE **and Nature**

Modern science provides powerful confirmations of the Law of Unity.

QUANTUM ENTANGLEMENT – Particles separated by vast distances respond to each other instantaneously, demonstrating that physical separation is an illusion.

THE ECOSYSTEM PRINCIPLE – Nature thrives through balance and interdependence. Every species, from the smallest microbe to the largest mammal, plays a role in sustaining the whole.

HUMAN BIOCHEMISTRY – The same elements that compose the stars—carbon, oxygen, hydrogen—form the human body, reinforcing that all things originate from the same source.

The harmony of the cosmos reflects the unity of all things. Just as galaxies move in synchronized rhythms, so too do human lives flow in unseen patterns of connection.

• See the Divine in all things – Recognize that God exists in every person, every animal, every element of creation.

• Practice love and forgiveness – By uplifting others, you uplift yourself and the entire web of existence.

• Engage in selfless service – Acts of kindness strengthen the unity of the whole.

• Meditate on oneness – Take moments to reflect on your connection to all things, dissolving the illusion of separation.

When one fully embraces the Law of Unity, life becomes a harmonious dance with the Divine. Conflict fades, fear diminishes, and love flows freely.

LAW 3: **The Law of Presence—Everything Is Here and Now**

THE ETERNAL NOW AND **the Illusion of Time**

At the core of existence lies a profound truth: the only reality is the present moment. The past is memory, the future is projection, but the now is where all experience unfolds. Time and space, as we perceive them, are merely constructs—tools consciousness uses to organize experience into comprehensible sequences.

Yet beyond human perception, something extraordinary is true:

everything that has ever existed and will ever exist is occurring in the eternal now. Modern physics, ancient spirituality, and divine wisdom all converge on this singular revelation. What we experience as time is simply consciousness moving through an eternal moment, creating the illusion of sequence and progression.

THE TRUTH **Behind Time**

Here's what this really means: We are all experiencing the same moment, but from different vantage points, which makes it appear as different moments. These vantage points are frequencies, determined by our state of being. Like multiple viewers watching the same movie from different timestamps, we're all in the same eternal now, just focused on different aspects of it.

From God's perspective—which is total omnipresence—past, present, and future exist as one. The Divine doesn't remember yesterday or await tomorrow; It experiences all of creation as a singular, eternal unfolding. Every possibility, every outcome, every moment already exists in this divine simultaneity.

Consider a filmstrip: all frames exist at once, yet we experience them sequentially as the projector moves through them. Reality operates similarly—all moments exist simultaneously, and our consciousness moves through this eternal framework, selecting experiences based on our perception, focus, and belief.

THE POWER **of This Understanding**

When you truly grasp this law, everything changes:

• The past exists only as memory, and the future exists only as possibility

• All healing, creation, and transformation happen in the present moment

• By focusing on the now, we access infinite potential and divine power

This understanding liberates us from the prison of linear thinking. Past regrets lose their grip because the past isn't "back there"—it's a frequency you're no longer tuned to. Future anxieties dissolve because the future isn't "ahead"—it's a potential waiting to be selected through your present state of being.

LIVING **in the Eternal Now**

This law calls us to awaken to the power of presence. Only in the now does divine transformation occur. Only here do healing, creation, and enlightenment unfold. When we fully embrace this moment, we align ourselves with the infinite intelligence that governs all existence. We stop living in the shadows of memory or the mirages of anticipation and start living where God's power flows most freely—right here, right now.

THE ULTIMATE REVELATION

You are the Infinite playing hide and seek with Itself. You hid your own divinity behind the veil of limitation—not to be lost, but to be found again. So that through the rediscovery of who you truly are, the Divine could awaken to itself in new, never-before-felt ways.

And when your earthly chapter ends, nothing is wasted. Every joy, every pain, every insight is absorbed back into the eternal field of knowing—what many call the Akashic Records. Your story becomes a living testament added to the library of God, expanding the wisdom of All That Is—forever.

THE **Doorway**

"Be still and know." When you stop seeking God in movement and meet God in stillness, when you cease becoming and rest in being, when you release all doing and dissolve into presence—the doorway opens, and you realize you've been standing in the Holy of Holies all along.

LAW 4: **The Law of Reflection—What You Put Out Is What You Get Back**

THE UNIVERSE **as a Mirror**

You are not living IN reality—you are creating it, moment by moment, through every thought, feeling, and belief you hold.

The universe functions as a vast, intelligent mirror, faithfully reflecting your internal state back to you as external experience. This isn't metaphor—it's the operating principle of existence. Fear breeds fearful circumstances. Love attracts loving experiences. Scarcity consciousness creates lack. Abundance mindset generates prosperity.

The world you see is not separate from you; it is an externalization of your internal landscape. You are not a passive observer but an active creator, constantly transmitting an energetic signal that reality mirrors back with absolute precision.

THE DIVINE MIRROR

"As a man thinketh in his heart, so is he." – Proverbs 23:7

From the divine perspective, God operates as an unconditionally loving mirror—no judgment, no preference, only perfect reflection. The Divine doesn't force outcomes upon you but reflects your consciousness through life's experiences. Jesus taught this principle: "A good tree cannot bear bad fruit, nor can a bad tree bear good fruit" (Matthew 7:18). The energy you emit determines the reality you experience.

Consider a physical mirror: It doesn't judge your appearance; it simply reflects. If you frown, it frowns back. No amount of pleading with the mirror will change the reflection—you must change yourself first. You cannot reach into the mirror to fix your hair; you fix it in reality, and the reflection follows instantly.

THIS IS THE FUNDAMENTAL TRUTH:

LIFE DOES NOT GIVE **you what you desire—it gives you what you ARE.**
- Persist in fear, receive fearful experiences
- Persist in love, receive love
- Persist in lack, experience scarcity
- Persist in gratitude, experience abundance

NOTHING IS FORCED UPON YOU. You choose your state, and the universe faithfully reflects it. This IS unconditional love—the Divine allowing you complete freedom to create your experience. You hold absolute power to shape your world through the frequency you emanate.

LET'S **Go Deeper**

I believe it's important to introduce a crucial concept here as we begin to work with this principle. For context, Abraham, a channeled guide that transmits through Esther Hicks, explains it like this:

The brain is a transmitting/receiving station. There are two signals being transmitted. One signal is from our Source. Bashar calls this signal "Consciousness itself". This signal is constant. It is the creative signal that created you before this lifetime. It's your core frequency signature. Your "soul print." Your signature frequency. As everyone is slightly different and unique, each person's frequency is slightly different. However, you can easily feel how your frequency feels any time you want to feel it. Just take one minute here and now and think of something or someone you love.

Bingo. If you took a moment to perform this exercise, you feel the feeling of love, which is your core frequency. Unconditional Love, actually. Here are some other core frequencies that you can feel now to be in alignment with your true authentic self are:

Unconditional Love/Love, Peace/Stillness, Joy/Bliss, Appreciation, Gratitude, Freedom/Empowerment, Optimism, Curiosity, Excitement, Contentment/Satisfaction.

Abraham calls this your emotional guidance system. Meaning, if you use your own internal guidance to lock into the truth about you, you are operating in alignment. A person in alignment is stronger than a million people who are not.

The universe is always holding this core frequency about you, and when you tap into any of these emotions they feel good, because it feels like home. Yes, feeling good feels like home. Yes, that's why feeling good feels good. Because it's your true core frequency. So connecting with your true self is like plugging yourself into Source. The ultimate charger and plug. True Power.

So when we use reality to think thoughts that are not vibrationally high, or thoughts that are contrary to who and what we truly are, yep, you guessed it. You feel bad. Or you pinch yourself off from Source. Honestly, you feel bad because you cut yourself off from Source, not because someone stole your dog, or you lost your keys. We often use "the thing" that happened as the excuse; however, as we elevate, we begin to see beyond appearances to what is truly going on. It all starts within.

Also, you can never be disconnected from God, although you can create the illusion of it in your reality. Again, you are God. You are using your power to create to generate a reality in which you feel disconnected. This is how much you are loved. God loves you so much that you are allowed to create a reality in which you consider yourself disconnected. And the irony in that is that you have to have power to create a reality, and this power comes from your connection to the Divine.

Abraham says that deciding whether or not to be connected is the highest priority decision you can ever make. It's a daily, moment by moment system. It decides if you are living empowered, through connection or allowing circumstances to cause you to choose disconnection or disempowerment.

This literally means that your emotions are your in-the-moment indicator of how your current thought aligns—or doesn't align—with the thoughts that Source is thinking about the same subject in this very moment. -Abraham Hicks

Ok, back to the point. Free Will.

There are two signals. One is emitted by your will, your state of being, your thoughts, your emotions. The other is the true signal that Source is emitting about you. When your signal matches Source's signal, you feel good. When you are out of alignment, you feel bad. It's that simple.

Let's be clear: Source is always emitting a good signal about you. Source always has an opinion about whatever you are having an opinion about—no matter how small. So it's always our responsibility to decide how we tune. We choose whether to tune into the truth of us or tune somewhere else—that's the nature of free will.

It's our choice how we tune. It's our choice how we think. It's our choice what state of being we embody.

LET'S get some Bible on this.

Jesus said, "Seek ye first the kingdom of God and his righteousness, and all these things shall be added unto you."

What he was saying was to "seek ye first the understanding, the knowing, that "You and the Father are one." You are God. We know this is true, as the Bible said he was the first born, so if he's our big brother, the first born with Christ consciousness, meaning a true knowing of who he was, then there are others being born everyday, as they awaken to the truth. This is the second coming of christ, the awakening to our oneness with God.

And his righteousness. The Righteousness of God is simply saying what God says about you. God, as we indicated before, only is holding your true core frequency. In Joel 3:10 God said let the weak say what? I am strong. Why?. "Let the weak say I am strong" reveals that God always holds the vision of our true, eternal strength—no matter our current struggle. This understanding applies to all areas of life—health, wealth, identity—by reminding us to speak not from our lack, but from our divine truth. It invites us to align our words with how God sees us: already whole, already powerful, already victorious. That frequency is only and always saying things like: You are love. You are the beloved. You are supported. You are backed up. You are health. You are wealthy. You are wise. I got you.

So the righteousness of God is only saying what God says about you. I am safe. I am secure. I am loved. I am blessed. I am wealthy. I am healthy. I am wise.

The deeper your belief goes, these affirmations will become incantations as your roots deepen, and your knowing anchors. As you do, you will tune your frequency to your highest timeline and begin to experience "all these things being added unto you." It is Divine Law. Your resonance changes to your authentic frequency. You are home, and once you awaken, you shall never sleep again.

When you truly seek first the Kingdom—that deep inner knowing of your oneness with God—and align with His righteousness by declaring the truth He already knows about you, you begin to resonate at the frequency of your divine nature. This isn't wishful thinking or empty affirmations. It's embodying the truth itself: actually feeling loved, whole, strong, abundant. From this state of being, you become a magnet for everything aligned with your highest good. As you become the vibration, all things are effortlessly added—because they were always yours.

. . .

UNDERSTANDING YOUR CREATIVE AUTHORITY: **The Three Levels of Reality**

To fully grasp why the universe mirrors your consciousness, we must understand the multi-layered nature of your divine identity. You are not simply receiving reflections—you are creating them through three simultaneous levels of being:

LEVEL 1: **You ARE God Experiencing Itself as You**

At the ultimate level, there is only One Consciousness, and you are That, having a localized experience through the lens of your individual perspective. You voluntarily forgot your true nature to embark on this journey of rediscovery. The separation you experience is intentional—a divine game of hide-and-seek where God hides its own divinity within the illusion of limitation, only to experience the joy of remembering itself through your awakening. This is why the universe reflects you perfectly—it IS you, reflecting yourself back to yourself.

LEVEL 2: **You Are a Holographic Fragment Containing the Whole**

Like a piece of a hologram that contains the entire image, you contain all of God's creative power and qualities, though currently filtered through your four-dimensional awareness. You're not a piece broken off from God; you're God focused through a specific lens.

Your oversoul simultaneously experiences multiple incarnations, and there are layers upon layers of consciousness extending back to Source. Yet even in this localized experience, you retain access to the whole—which is why miracles are possible and why consciousness can transcend apparent limitations.

LEVEL 3: **You Are Sovereign Creator of Your Reality**

At the practical level of daily experience, you operate with creative authority in multiple realms:

• YOUR PERSONAL REALITY: Here you are absolute creator. Every person you encounter is YOUR version of them—a reflection cast by your consciousness. This is why the same person can appear loving in one person's reality and harsh in another's. You're not meeting "them"—you're meeting your reflection of them.

• THE COLLECTIVE REALITY: You also participate in a consensus reality where all aspects of God collectively agree on certain parameters—physical laws, shared events, common timelines. Here, you have co-creative influence. Think of it as a cosmic democracy where your vote (your consciousness) contributes to the collective experience.

• THE INTERSECTION: Your personal reality overlays the collective reality. When ten people witness the same event, there are actually ten different events occurring in ten personal realities, with enough agreement to maintain collective coherence.

WHY THIS CHANGES **Everything**

Understanding these layers transforms how you work with the Law of Reflection:

1. **Personal Relationships:** That difficult person in your life? They're showing up that way in YOUR reality because they're reflecting something within you. Change your inner state, and watch

how they transform in your experience—while potentially remaining unchanged in someone else's reality.

2. **World Events:** While you participate in collective agreements about major events, HOW they impact you and WHAT they mean in your reality is entirely your creation. This is why the same event can be devastating to one person and liberating to another.

3. **Your Power:** You're not a small being hoping to influence a large universe. You're the universe itself, experiencing your own creative power through the focused lens of your individual perspective. The reflection isn't happening TO you—it's happening AS you.

THE PRACTICAL APPLICATION

When you understand that you're both the creator and the creation, the projector and the screen, the mirror and the reflection, you stop trying to change the mirror and start changing what's being reflected. You recognize that:

• At the deepest level, there's only One here, and it's You/God/All That Is

• At the practical level, you have complete authority over your personal experience

• At the collective level, you contribute to humanity's shared journey

This is why "It's All U" operates on every level—because whether we're talking about your personal reality, the collective experience, or ultimate truth, it all comes back to consciousness experiencing itself through infinite perspectives, and you ARE that consciousness.

The universe doesn't reflect your small self's desires—it reflects your true state of being. And as you remember more of who you really are, your reflection becomes increasingly aligned with the divine truth: You are God, exploring your own infinite nature through the beautiful illusion of being you.

This section bridges the theological understanding with the practical application of the Law of Reflection, making clear why the universe reflects our consciousness while acknowledging the multi-layered nature of reality creation.

THE SCIENCE CONFIRMS **the Scripture**

Modern physics validates ancient wisdom:

• **Quantum Observer Effect:** Consciousness literally affects the behavior of particles, proving that observation shapes reality

• **Neuroplasticity:** Your brain rewires itself based on repeated thoughts, creating patterns that influence perception and behavior

• **Resonance:** Like frequencies attract—your vibrational state magnetically draws matching experiences

THE BUFFER **of Grace**

This reflection isn't instant—there's a merciful delay between thought and manifestation. As Abraham-Hicks explains, sustained thoughts gain momentum: hold a thought for 15 seconds, and similar thoughts join it, building creative power every 15 seconds thereafter. This buffer allows us to course-correct before thoughts fully manifest. It's why we experience linear time—to witness our choices, learn, and consciously create rather than instantly manifest every passing thought.

THE ULTIMATE TRUTH

You are the sole authority in your reality. Everything you perceive—every person, every experience, every circumstance—is your consciousness reflected back through different lenses, different angles, different frequencies. What you see around you isn't separate from you; it's simply another version of you, viewed from a different perspective.

In a world of external noise—social media, comparison, outside validation—remember: we live in an inside-out reality. True power comes from aligning with your authentic frequency, not performing for approval. You're not separate from the universe; you are its reflection.

This isn't unique to you. It's the truth for every being in existence. And as your awareness expands—bit by bit—you begin to see this grand interconnectedness. The more you include, the more you become aware of.

As you raise your frequency—what many call ascension—others call it enlightenment—you begin to realize something profound. Even at the highest peak of that journey, you will find only one thing.

You.

More of you.

Because you ARE it.

To change your life, change your reflection. To change your reflection, change within.

It's All U.

LAW 5: **The Law of Change—Everything Changes Except the Five Laws**

THE ETERNAL DANCE **of Transformation**

Change is the only constant in the universe. From the birth of galaxies to the seasons of the Earth, from the ebb and flow of human emotions to the shifting tides of time, everything is in a continuous state of transformation. Yet, amidst this eternal motion, Five immutable laws remain steadfast. These laws—Eternal Existence, Unity, Presence, Reflection, and Change—form the foundation of reality. They govern existence across dimensions, ensuring that while all things evolve, the divine structure of creation remains intact. Change itself is a sacred expression of God's infinite creativity, an ever-unfolding masterpiece in which every moment is a brushstroke on the canvas of eternity. By understanding the Law of Change, we move beyond resistance and fear. We learn to embrace transformation as an essential and divine process. And in doing so, we align ourselves with the natural rhythm of the universe—one that does not fight against change, but flows harmoniously with it.

THE DIVINE FOUNDATION **of Change**

"Behold, I make all things new." – Revelation 21:5

Change is not random. It is not chaotic. It is divinely orchestrated, a function of God's omnipotence and omniscience. Everything shifts, grows, and evolves, but never outside of divine order. Even the stars are not eternal in form—they are born, they burn, they collapse, and yet the essence of their energy remains, transformed into new forms. This is the divine dance of existence—eternal transformation within eternal constancy.

THE SACRED PURPOSE **of Change in Human Experience**

For humans, change often feels threatening because it challenges the illusion of control. We cling to familiar patterns, relationships, and circumstances, fearing that transformation will lead to loss. Yet, the Law of Change reveals that resistance to transformation is resistance to life itself.

Change serves several divine purposes:

1. Personal Growth and Evolution – Every challenge becomes a catalyst that propels us toward greater understanding and expanded capability.

2. Consciousness Expansion – New experiences continuously broaden our awareness and deepen our spiritual wisdom.

3. Truth Alignment – Transformation strips away illusions and reveals what is genuinely real and lasting.

4. Divine Creative Expression – Through change, we actively participate in the ongoing creation of reality itself.

When we align with the Law of Change, we discover that transformation is not something that happens to us—it is something we participate in consciously. Life is happening for you.

EMBRACING **Change as Divine Will**

"To every thing there is a season, and a time to every purpose under the heaven." – Ecclesiastes 3:1

The Bible acknowledges that change is not only natural but necessary. Each season serves a purpose, and resistance to seasonal change would be futile and destructive. Similarly, the changes in our lives—whether welcomed or unwelcome—serve divine purposes that may not be immediately apparent. By trusting the process and maintaining faith in divine order, we can navigate change with grace and wisdom. Later we will discuss the proper perspective to have when change appears. It has been very useful in my life.

THE PARADOX **of Constancy Within Change**

While everything changes, the Five Laws themselves remain constant. This creates a fascinating paradox: within the flow of endless transformation, there exists an unchanging foundation. This foundation provides stability and security even as everything else shifts.

Understanding this paradox allows us to:

• Find peace in uncertainty, knowing that divine laws remain constant

• Trust the process of change, recognizing it as part of divine order

• Maintain our center while adapting to new circumstances

• See change as an expression of divine creativity rather than chaos

THE POWER **of Perspective in Change**

One of the most profound aspects of the Law of Change is that we have the power to determine the meaning of every transformation. While we cannot always control what happens, we can always control how we interpret and respond to what happens.

This power of perspective is divine authority in action. By choosing to see every event—even seemingly negative ones—as a pathway to greater good, we align ourselves with the highest possible outcome.

The Bible confirms this principle in Romans 8:28: "And we know that all things work together for good to those who love God, to those who are called according to His purpose."

By standing in divine authority and choosing to see everything as beneficial, you align yourself with the highest possible outcome.

CONCLUSION: **Change as Your Divine Ally**

The Law of Change is not meant to disrupt you—it is meant to empower you. When you accept that you control the meaning of every experience, you unlock true freedom.

• Every challenge can be transformed into a stepping stone

• Every event is an opportunity to elevate your frequency

• You are the divine force in your own experience

When you declare your reality and trust the universal laws, life begins to unfold with effortless grace. Embrace your power, and let the universe mirror it back to you.

And so, we trust. We declare. We align with the highest truth: All things are working in our favor.

CHAPTER 2 KEY TAKEAWAYS:

• Each of the Five Laws operates continuously in your life, whether you're aware of them or not

• The Law of Reflection shows you that reality mirrors your internal state back to you

• Understanding these laws transforms you from victim to conscious creator

• When you align with these principles, life flows with divine ease and synchronicity

THREE

CHAPTER 3: THE GOOD STUFF - LET'S MAKE TOAST!!!

We have finally gotten to what I would call the good stuff! To be honest, all of this book is good stuff to me, because I am certainly a very curious creature and need to know how things work. This book up until now, is full of Divine Universal Laws, full of understanding about who you are, how you came to be, the purpose of life etc. But now we are getting to the good part! From this point forward, we will provide techniques and insights that you can use in physical, practical ways to elevate your life. How does all this information affect how you live your daily life. What is the advantage of knowing this information. What good is all this spiritual "woo woo" anyway? One last analogy before we dig in. Abraham once said something to the effect that, "You don't have to know how electricity works in order to make toast". You can just plug in the toaster, pop some bread in, adjust the settings, press a button and "voila" toast! This is akin to this chapter vs the previous information in this book. You don't have to know about all the spiritual laws in order to live an effective life. Will that information help? Yes tremendously, as you will apply the information in this chapter with more certainty because you understand the laws. Is it required that you understand it? Nope. You can just begin to incorporate the techniques in this chapter and beyond into your life and your life will begin to improve! Yep Your welcome in advance! God is the Dopest!

UNDERSTANDING **Your Divine Worthiness**

So from my perspective as a technical engineer, it's important to understand the order of how things work. So with that, it was important to lay the foundational groundwork about existence itself so that you can see your place in life. Now that we've established the Five Laws of the Universe (as explored in Chapters 1-2), we can apply this divine framework to transform your daily experience. Hopefully by the time you have gotten here you understand better about your worthiness. This is important because simply put, without "YOU". All that is would not be all that is! The supreme intelligence doesn't make mistakes, so if you exist, you are needed. In this "neediness", is your worthiness. You are so worthy that for All That Is to be complete, you were created. The specific aspect of the divine that you represent, is a cause for celebration. No one has your "soul print". This is a concept that is like a fingerprint, but is composed of your vibration make-up, personality, gifts, dreams, what makes "you" uniquely you. No one else is YOU. You are a unique aspect of divine intelligence. You have a specific frequency, unlike anyone else. You have a specific mathematical equation that delineates who you are from another being. You have a specific chemical make-up that sets you apart from another. You are not merely in the universe, the universe is within you. In this unique aspect of God is held your value. How much value do you put on GOD? How much is GOD worth? What's the worth of the Divine? This worth is also your value, as you are god in human form. From this you can see that worthiness is something that comes from spiritual understanding first, before it enters the natural. So without having a firm understanding on who you are, many people won't allow the abundance that is their birthright to come in the various ways that it could. Actually all of your stuff so to speak is coming to you every day in every way. You are literally the only obstacle blocking it from entering your awareness. Your perception, your reality. You are the only one not allowing yourself to perceive it. The divine has already said YES! As Abraham would say. You are holding the umbrella up preventing the blessing from entering into your life. This book is designed to bring you back to remembrance of who you truly are, so you can let down your umbrella, and feel the rain of your blessings showering down upon you. My hope is that you know your worthiness, remember who you are, and allow all your stuff in—in perfect order—knowing it's supposed to be this way.

THE RULES **of the Game Called Life**

Myles Munroe has some magnificent teachings on being a "Kingdomaire." In order to explain things properly, this will be a comprehensive approach to the rules of this game called life.

Notice: I will say the same things over and over in different ways, intentionally providing different approaches for you to glean from. This is with blistering intention—this is your life! How well do you do at a video game when you first begin versus the 100th time you've played? How well do you do when you've just jumped in versus the 100th time, when you've figured out the rules and where the pitfalls are? Yes, exactly.

Think of this information as a guide—as the cheat code. It's comprehensive, but is it the only way? Nope! It's the way I've found that works for me to understand what is going on. Must you believe it? Nope! You can carve out your own way; that's totally acceptable. This is strictly what works for me, and I wanted to help others. So I'm detailing the information in a hopefully digestible format so others may catch it quicker, sooner, and know how to apply it for personal success.

I'm also intentionally looping in the biblical aspect of things, as I know many people grew up in the church on certain "Christian concepts." I want to draw a correlation to how these laws actually work and play into the entire scene of reality. Quite frankly, what good is spiritual text if it's not applicable in daily life?

In order to "win" at life, you first need to know what the rules are. And therein lies the issue: We haven't been given an accurate rulebook that allows us to play with our full potential. We haven't been able to see or understand what life is supposed to really be about. Sure, we watch our star athletes, our movie stars, wealthy people, even our religious leaders—hoping to piece together the picture for ourselves. But what is the goal here? What is the aim?

Am I supposed to be going after as much money as I can get? Is the aim to be with as many men or women as humanly possible? Is the goal to make everyone else think like I do? What is the goal?

So after leaving the biblical text alone for quite a while (Bible's Instructions: Basic Instructions Before Leaving Earth) and looking into more spiritual teachings, I was able to see more clearly what Jesus was actually speaking about.

NOW LET'S **PROVIDE SOME CONTEXT**

Here is a basic mathematical equation, a basic scientific equations, along with the individuals who formulated or contributed to them. We also have a Linux Grep command, and a GIT Command. No this isn't a test by far. This is just an example of formulas that has been widely accepted and used around the world daily for calculations in their respective fields. What does this mean. This means that While I didn't invent "GREP/ OR GIT", I use these commands daily in my job and I dare say would not be able to do my job effectively without them. The same goes for the Spiritual equations and Formula's that I'm going to provide in this chapter. While, I didn't invent these formulas or equations, I use them daily, and with an understanding of this information you too will be able to "MAKE TOAST" without burning it!

. . .

MATHEMATICAL EQUATIONS:

1. **Pythagorean Theorem**
  ◦ Inventor: Pythagoras (c. 570–495 BCE)
  ◦ $a^2 + b^2 = c^2$
  ◦ Description: This theorem states that in a right-angled triangle, the square of the length of the hypotenuse (c) equals the sum of the squares of the lengths of the other two sides (a and b).

SCIENTIFIC EQUATIONS:

2. **Einstein's Mass-Energy Equivalence**
  ◦ Inventor: Albert Einstein (1879–1955)
  ◦ $E = mc^2$
  ◦ Description: This equation from Einstein's Special Theory of Relativity expresses that energy (E) is equal to mass (m) multiplied by the square of the speed of light (c), demonstrating the interconversion of mass and energy.

3. **LINUX GREP**
  • Inventor: Ken Thompson
  • Year: 1973
  Also look at the following complex grep:

```
GREP -EO '[0-9]{4}-[0-9]{2}-[0-9]{2} [0-9]{2}:[0-9]{2}:[0-9]{2}' app.log | awk -v today="$(date '+%Y-%m-%d')" '$1 == today' | sed 's/-/\//g'
```
```
` ` `
```

· · ·

THIS COMMAND FINDS all timestamps in a log file (app.log), extracts only those from the last 24 hours, and reformats them into a human-readable format.

4. **Complex git Command**
    - Inventor: Linus Torvalds
    - YEAR 2005

REWRITING Commit History for a Specific Author

```
GIT FILTER-BRANCH --env-filter '
    if [ "$GIT_AUTHOR_EMAIL" = "old.email@example.com" ]
    then
    export GIT_AUTHOR_NAME="New Name"
    export GIT_AUTHOR_EMAIL="new.email@example.com"
    fi
    ' --tag-name-filter cat -- --all
```

THIS COMMAND CHANGES the author of all commits where a specific old email was used.

LET'S **Get to the Point:**
Just as I didn't invent the Pythagorean theorem, Einstein's $E=mc^2$, or the GREP and GIT commands that I use daily as an engineer, I also didn't create the spiritual formulas and concepts that I'm about to share with you. But here's the thing—these mathematical and technical equations have become foundational understandings in their respective fields because they work. When engineers need to calculate structural integrity, we use $a^2 + b^2 = c^2$. When physicists

explore the relationship between mass and energy, they turn to $E = mc^2$. When I need to extract specific data from log files or manage code repositories, I rely on GREP and GIT commands that have been proven effective for decades.

Similarly, the spiritual teachers like Abraham and Bashar, have provided core concepts, formulas, and equations for viewing and approaching life that serve as foundational understandings in the realm of consciousness and spiritual mastery. Just as these mathematical and technical formulas can lead to success in engineering and science, these spiritual principles can lead to success and victory in life itself. I may not have invented them, but I use them daily because they produce results. And once you understand these spiritual equations, you too will have access to the same foundational tools that can transform your reality from the inside out.

My personal journey is exactly that, a bridge, as I firsthand have gone from a state of chaos to Divine knowing through the understanding provided in this book. I am not suggesting that my way is the only way, nor do I wish for people to look to me. I am merely a sign post indicating that the way that I went worked for me to come into my mastery, Or my becoming, as I'm still learning, improving and growing. I understand that there is no 'right' way contrary to popular belief. I even understand that no one is wrong on the way that they are choosing. I'm simply saying with this information, that I wanted to go this way because this is the life that I choose to live, once I had a chance to review all that was available to me to live. This is what I choose to do with my energy and my time. Take whatever you can use for your journey.

Spiritual Freedom is freedom of the soul. The freedom to choose my thoughts. The freedom to choose my reactions to any situation. The freedom and power to choose my point of attraction. The freedom to define circumstances in my reality in a way that is empowering. The freedom that comes from my divine knowing is everything.

· · ·

THE DIVINE CREATION STORY **& The Purpose of Life**

EARTH AS A MASTER **Class**

"You won the lottery. You have a body." —Theo

Earth is not a place of punishment nor a mere coincidence—it is a master class, a divine school where souls refine their ability to manifest, awaken to their divine nature, and exercise their true power. Before entering this life, you knew yourself as divine, limitless, and eternal, but in order to truly experience growth, you chose to forget. The agreement was made: You would be "born into sin and raised in darkness," not as a curse but as a path to rediscover your own greatness. Yes, "you are not on a path, You Are the Path" (Bashar). This echoes throughout sacred teachings in Jeremiah 1:5: "Before I formed thee in the belly I knew thee; and before thou camest forth out of the womb I sanctified thee." Jesus was not an exception—he was the example. He remembered his divine nature and showed that every soul has the capacity to step into divine knowing.

Let me provide a personal example about the curriculum of the master class. One challenge that I had to apply the understanding I explain in Divine Knowing came when dealing with the birth of my youngest son. He was born autistic due to a birth injury. As you can imagine it was a very difficult time in our lives as we initially had envisioned having a healthy baby boy. Even up until the delivery room, we had no idea that our lives was about to change.

Needless to say after spending 6 weeks in the NICU, complete with round the clock visits, kangaroo care, and a lot of tears we finally got to take our son home. The battle however wasn't over and it would be 3-4 more years before we even had a chance to breathe or relax. Our son was born with a birth injury, and labeled autistic. Very new to this and without warning we were thrust into the chaos of adapting.

I can hear Abraham saying her famous saying that "Alignment isn't like a college degree, meaning once you get it you're all set. It's a day by day choice that you have to choose". Our world was shattered, not only because our picture perfect family was destroyed, but because we were thrown this curve ball of which there was no coming back from. This wasn't a 10 year thing and things would change back. This was a permanent shift in life.

Well needless to say, I wanted answers and clarity on why this had happened, and what did this mean. All I could remember, was that all of our pre-natal visits were excellent, and we had followed all of the doctors orders and "WHAM", out of the blue we were smacked upside the head with this life altering curve ball.

Well it wasn't until many, many years later, did I come across Bashar's teaching on earth being a Master Class, and the concept of each person picking your parents as well as your challenges to learn certain lessons. See Bashar's take was before coming to earth we decide who our parents are, or what their basic make-up would be. We choose the circumstances with which we would be born, in effect as our classroom of subject matter to deal with and overcome or transmute from darkness into light. He said that earth was the toughest school, and was considered to be a master class, not only because of the subject matter, but because we had chosen to forget who we are, and were.

He indicated that often times people on this earth who were considered to be special needs, were highly advanced spiritual teachers in spirit, who had intentionally chosen to be born with the extreme limitation of their "handicap", or "disability", in order to have an extreme focus and to compound burning through lifetimes of "karma" at once. He went on to say, that these agreements were made long before coming into this earth plane, and that there were no accidents.

That meant that I was free to stop blaming the doctors and the hospital for what I considered to be extreme malpractice. I could stop blaming the lawyers who indicated that although they agreed that we had a case, it would be difficult to prosecute, because our son "looked too normal" to garner sympathy from the jury. I could stop blaming

"God", for this punishment, as a victim, and begin to look at this from a new angle.

How do you go from praying and declaring a happy healthy birth, to sitting in the pre-natal ICU, just like that? When the lawyers investigated the case, he basically indicated that the doctors and nurses involved must have concocted their story of what occurred because all the timestamps of what occurred lined up perfectly to within the law. He said in his 30 years of practicing law, he had never seen this before!

Healing and forgiveness is not for the weak, let's just say that, and it wasn't until some 4-5 years after my son was born, that I found understanding to begin my healing journey. It's one thing to teach about love and forgiveness, it's a totally new thing to have to do it. Even harder when you feel you have been wronged with no apology. Even harder still with something that will affect you and even worse your child for the rest of their life.

Well needless to say, Bashar's explanation of how our soul contracts work, was pivotal to my freedom. Dolores Cannon's explanation, as well as Abraham's wisdom on the subject of pre-life choice, the eternalness of life, and soul contracts were pivotal to my freedom around this subject. Today I regard my son as one of my great spiritual teachers. He has shown me so much, and continues to help me grow and mature in the things that truly matter.

THE JOURNEY IS **the Purpose**

"The purpose of life is not a destination; it is the process itself. It's the lived experience. What you become in the process. The remembering, the awakening, the tuning. It's the alchemy of turning the darkness into light as you transcend your circumstances through enlightenment. Many seek a singular, grand purpose, yet the purpose of life is the journey itself—the continual unfolding of self-realization. You are not meant to "find" your purpose as though it were a hidden object. Rather, you are meant to live in alignment with your highest excitement in each moment. To be yourself as fully as you can, the best you know how—that is the mission. That is the purpose. That's it." Every challenge, every obstacle, every death is a change in perspective, not an end to who we are.

YOU ARE NOT **a Body with a Soul—You are a Soul with a Body**

We do not "have" a soul; we are the soul. The physical body exists within the soul, not the other way around. The soul contracts itself into a focus—a crystallized "seed" as Bashar explains it—to experience physical reality. When physical life ends, the seed expands again, reintegrating into the broader awareness of the soul. Think of your soul like a vast ocean, and your physical body as a small cup of that water. The cup may appear separate, but it is still made of the same ocean. When the cup is emptied, the water returns to the whole.

THE UNIVERSE AS A MIRROR: **Reflection of Your Consciousness**

The fundamental principle underlying physical reality is that it does not exist independently; it is only a projection, a reflection of your consciousness. The external world you experience is a mirror—an exact reflection of the definitions and beliefs you hold within yourself. "Physical reality isn't real on its own. It's only the product of what you define it to be." (Bashar) This means that the experiences and circumstances you encounter are not random. They are a direct feedback loop—a mirror reflecting what you believe, what you expect, and how you define yourself. When you seek to change your external reality, the true transformation does not come from altering the reflection directly but from changing the source—your consciousness. "Just because the reflection is frowning, that doesn't prevent me from deciding to smile. I can just decide to smile. And when I do, the reflection will have no choice but to smile back." (Bashar) This realization is empowering because it places the full creative authority within you. You are not at the mercy of circumstances; instead, the circumstances are a neutral reflection of your internal state.

THE DIVINE BEING'S IMPARTIALITY: **Absolute Neutrality**

The universe or the divine consciousness is not judging your choices, no matter what they are. "Reality", in its true form, is neutral —a set of props that gain meaning only through the definitions you assign to them. "You now know that things on the outside are just neutral props, devoid of meaning, with no built-in meaning. You determine the meaning." (Bashar) This neutrality means that the universe is not punishing or rewarding you. It is simply responding to the vibrations you emit based on your definitions and emotional states. For example, if you experience the same challenges over and over again, it does not necessarily mean life is against you. Instead, it means you are interpreting those challenges in a way that reinforces them. The moment you define those experiences differently—as opportunities for growth, clarity, or expansion—they will begin to shift. This is why conviction is key. The first stage of truly knowing that you have changed is when you respond differently to the same situation than you did before. If you react the same way, you reinforce the same reality. But if you approach it with a new understanding, a new belief, a new frequency, reality must adjust accordingly. "By responding differently to the same situation, you give the situation leave to truly reflect the change within you." (Bashar) This neutrality of the divine being and the universe also means no external force is holding you back—only your own internalized agreements with limiting beliefs.

THE FOURTH LAW: **What You Put Out Is What You Get Back**

One of the five fundamental laws of the universe is: What you put out is what you get back. This is not just about action; it is about vibration, definition, and belief. The frequency you hold within yourself is the only thing reality can reflect back to you. If you change your frequency, your external world must reflect that change. "The measure of change is not when the outside changes. The measure of change is that you respond differently to the outside even if it still looks the same." (Bashar) This is the most challenging aspect of change—understanding that your inner shift comes first, and only when it is complete will external changes become visible. If you are waiting for the outside to change before you feel different, you haven't truly changed. "As soon as you actually stop caring whether the outside changes to match the things you prefer, then because that's a true change, the outside will have no choice but to change to reflect it." (Bashar) If you are acting from a place of scarcity, fear, or doubt, reality will reflect scarcity, fear, and doubt. If you instead embody abundance, trust, and certainty, the external world will mirror those states. This is why faith is not about waiting for proof—it is about being the proof. You must choose to define yourself as already being that which you desire, without demanding validation from external reality. "As long as you make the change within you conditional on the outside having to change to reflect it, that means you haven't changed, and therefore the outside never will." (Bashar)

FINAL INSIGHTS: **Mastering the Reflection**

1. Reality is a Mirror. You cannot manipulate the reflection without first changing what is being reflected.

2. The Universe is Neutral. It holds no preference for what you experience. It merely reflects your state of being.

3. You Are the Cause. Your beliefs, emotions, and vibrations dictate what you experience.

4. What You Put Out Is What You Get Back. If you truly change, your external world will follow—but only when you no longer need it to.

5. Unconditional Alignment. The paradox of manifestation is that you must first be what you desire before the world reflects it back.

THE ULTIMATE REALIZATION

"God is a mirror." (Bashar) The divine presence does not impose itself upon you—it simply reflects your consciousness back to you. When you truly understand this, you recognize that your freedom, your power, and your transformation are entirely within your hands.

YOUR DIVINE HIGHER **Guidance**

Building upon the foundation of the Five Laws, we now explore the practical application of divine knowing through what Bashar calls "The Formula for Acting on Your Highest Excitement." This formula is not merely a suggestion—it is the fundamental mechanism by which consciousness navigates reality in alignment with divine will. Your excitement is not random. It is not a fleeting emotion or a whimsical desire. It is the language of your Higher Mind, the voice of your soul, the compass that points toward your highest path. When you learn to follow this guidance system, life transforms from struggle to flow, from confusion to clarity, from limitation to infinite possibility.

UNDERSTANDING   **Excitement**   as   **Divine Communication**

Excitement is your unique vibrational signature—the frequency that represents your authentic self. It is how your Higher Mind communicates with your physical mind, guiding you toward experiences that serve your highest good and the expansion of consciousness itself. Think of excitement as a GPS system for the soul. Just as a GPS knows the optimal route to your destination, your excitement knows the optimal path to your highest expression. It takes into account factors that your logical mind cannot perceive—synchronicities, timing, other people's paths, and the greater unfolding of divine plan.

THE THREE-STEP FORMULA—BY **Bashar**

The formula for acting on your highest excitement consists of three essential components:

1. **Act on whatever excites you most in any given moment**

This means paying attention to what genuinely energizes you, what draws your interest, what feels alive and vibrant. It doesn't have to be a grand life purpose—it could be as simple as calling a friend, taking a walk, reading a book, or organizing your space. The key is to identify what carries the highest energy for you in this moment.

2. **Act on it to the best of your ability, taking it as far as you can**

This means giving your full presence and energy to whatever you're doing. Don't hold back, don't do things halfway. Of course, this will never cause you to do "Illegal" activities or harm someone else. Pursue the excitement with integrity and commitment until you either complete it or it naturally transforms into something else.

3. **Act with zero insistence on what the outcome should be**

This is perhaps the most challenging aspect for the physical mind. You must release attachment to specific results and trust that the process itself is guiding you perfectly. The Higher Mind sees the bigger picture that the physical mind cannot perceive.

Why This Formula Works

The formula works because it aligns you with the fundamental structure of existence. When you act on excitement, you are:

• Connecting to your Higher Mind's guidance system – Your excitement is literally your soul speaking to you

• Aligning with your soul's purpose and path – What excites you is always connected to your highest expression

• Operating from your natural frequency – This attracts harmonious experiences and synchronicities

• Becoming a co-creator with the universe – Rather than fighting against the flow, you're moving with it

THE INTELLIGENCE **of Excitement**

As you begin to act on your excitement you will find that the divine contains within it everything you need to know about timing, sequence, and direction. Acting on your excitement will trigger the other attributes that come into focus, every time you begin to physically act on your excitement or passion. It is a complete system that includes:

• The motivating force – It provides the energy and enthusiasm to take action

• The organizing principle – It arranges experiences in the most beneficial order

• The path of least resistance – It ensures you're always moving with the natural flow of your energy

• The connecting thread – It links seemingly unrelated experiences into a unified journey

• The revealing mirror – It exposes limiting beliefs so they can be acknowledged and transformed

PRACTICAL APPLICATION **of the Formula**

. . .

STARTING **Where You Are**

You don't need to wait for some grand revelation about your life purpose to begin applying this formula. Start exactly where you are, with whatever level of excitement you can access in this moment. If you're feeling stuck or uninspired, ask yourself:

- "What would I enjoy doing right now?"
- "What feels lighter or more energizing to me?"
- "If I had to choose between these options, which one has more aliveness to it?"

Even the smallest movement in the direction of excitement begins to activate the formula and create momentum.

RECOGNIZING **True Excitement vs. False Excitement**

True excitement has certain characteristics:

- It feels expansive and energizing
- It doesn't require you to harm yourself or others
- It feels authentic to who you are
- It often involves some element of growth or contribution
- It maintains its energy when you think about it

FALSE EXCITEMENT OFTEN INVOLVES:

- Addiction or compulsive behavior
- Escapism from responsibility
- Harm to yourself or others
- A desperate or needy quality
- Energy that quickly dissipates

WORKING **with Resistance**

When you begin following your excitement, you may encounter resistance in the form of fear, doubt, or limiting beliefs. This is normal and actually part of the process. The formula is designed to bring these limitations to the surface so they can be acknowledged and transformed.

When resistance arises:

• Acknowledge it without judgment – "I notice I'm feeling afraid about this"

• Investigate the belief behind it – "What would I have to believe for this fear to make sense?"

• Choose a more empowering perspective – "How could I reframe this in a way that serves me?"

• Take action anyway – Move forward despite the fear, knowing that action dissolves resistance

THE SYNCHRONISTIC NATURE **of Following Excitement**

When you consistently follow your excitement, you begin to notice that life becomes increasingly synchronistic. The right people appear at the right time. Opportunities open up in unexpected ways. Resources become available just when you need them. This is not coincidence—it is the natural result of aligning with the organizing intelligence of the universe. When you follow your excitement, you are following the same intelligence that orchestrates the movement of planets, the changing of seasons, and the beating of your heart.

COMMON   MISCONCEPTIONS   **About   Following Excitement**

"IT'S SELFISH"

Many people worry that following their excitement is selfish or irresponsible. In reality, the opposite is true. When you follow your authentic excitement, you become more energized, creative, and capable of contributing to others. You cannot give what you don't have, and following your excitement ensures that you're operating from a full cup rather than an empty one.

"IT'S IMPRACTICAL"

The physical mind often judges excitement as impractical because it cannot see the bigger picture. However, following excitement is actually the most practical thing you can do because it aligns you with the path of least resistance and maximum effectiveness.

"I DON'T KNOW **What Excites Me**"

If you feel disconnected from your excitement, start small. Pay attention to what feels slightly better, slightly more interesting, slightly more alive. As you practice following these subtle preferences, your connection to excitement will strengthen.

THE RELATIONSHIP BETWEEN **Excitement and Service**

True excitement always contains an element of service—not necessarily in an obvious way, but in the sense that when you express your authentic self, you contribute something unique to the world. Your excitement is not separate from your purpose; it is the pathway to discovering and expressing your purpose.

When you follow your excitement:
- You model authenticity for others
- You contribute your unique gifts to the world
- You raise the vibration of everyone around you
- You participate in the expansion of consciousness itself

CHAPTER 3 KEY TAKEAWAYS:
- The Five Laws and practical application ("making toast") transform theory into lived experience

• Your worthiness is inherent - you exist because you are needed by All That Is

• Earth is a Master Class where you chose to forget your divinity in order to remember it more fully

• Reality is a neutral mirror reflecting your consciousness back to you

• You hold complete creative authority over your experience through your definitions and beliefs

• Your excitement is divine guidance, not random emotion

• The three-step formula provides a practical method for aligning with your Higher Mind

• Following excitement leads to synchronicity and effortless manifestation

• Resistance is part of the process and helps reveal limiting beliefs

• True excitement always serves both your highest good and the good of the whole

FOUR

CHAPTER 4: THE MIRROR PRINCIPLE

Understanding Reality as Reflection

One of the most profound and transformative principles in Divine Knowing is the understanding that reality functions as a mirror. This is not metaphorical—it is the literal mechanism by which consciousness creates experience. Everything you encounter in your external world is a precise reflection of your internal state of being.

This principle revolutionizes how we understand personal responsibility, relationships, and the nature of reality itself. When you truly grasp that the outer world mirrors your inner world, you shift from being a victim of circumstances to being the conscious creator of your experience.

THE FUNDAMENTAL NATURE **of the Mirror**

"God is a mirror. It can only show you what you're giving off. That's all it can do." (Bashar)

Reality has no inherent nature of its own—it is neutral. Like a mirror, it simply reflects back what is presented to it. If you look into a physical mirror and see a frown, you don't try to change the reflection by reaching into the mirror. You change your expression, and the reflection automatically changes. Reality also has no built-in meaning. This means that any event can be positive, negative, or neutral, depending on the label you place upon it. This ties into the fourth law: what you put out, you get back. What you put out and define internally is reflected back to you. This principle affirms your power, as you get to define your reality and thus how it is experienced. Rev. Ike has a wonderful sermon that speaks about this, entitled "I meet no one but me."

The same principle applies to life. Your external circumstances are reflections of your internal definitions, beliefs, emotions, and vibrational state. To change your external reality, you must first change what you're projecting internally.

THE MECHANICS **of Reflection**

THE MIRROR PRINCIPLE operates through several mechanisms:

Vibrational Resonance – Everything in existence vibrates at specific frequencies. Your thoughts, emotions, and beliefs create a vibrational signature that attracts experiences of matching frequency.

Belief Confirmation – Reality organizes itself to confirm your beliefs about yourself and the world. If you believe life is difficult, you'll experience circumstances that validate that belief.

Emotional Magnetism – Your emotional state acts as a magnet, drawing experiences that match your predominant feelings.

Perceptual Filtering – Your consciousness filters reality to show you evidence that supports your existing worldview.

SELF-LOVE: **The Foundation of All Reflection**

. . .

THE MOST IMPORTANT relationship you have is with yourself, because it determines how all other relationships unfold. If you don't love yourself, you cannot truly love anyone else, and you cannot receive love from others in a way that feels authentic and fulfilling.

Self-love is not narcissism or selfishness—it is the recognition of your divine nature and inherent worth. When you love yourself, you:

- Accept yourself as you are while remaining open to growth
- Treat yourself with kindness and compassion
- Honor your needs and boundaries
- Celebrate your unique gifts and contributions
- Forgive yourself for past mistakes
- Trust in your inherent goodness and potential

THE SELF-LOVE REFLECTION **Cycle**

When you love yourself, reality reflects that love back to you in countless ways:

- People treat you with greater respect and kindness
- Opportunities align with your highest good
- Synchronicities increase dramatically
- Abundance flows more easily into your life
- Relationships become more harmonious and supportive

Conversely, when you don't love yourself, reality reflects that lack of self-love:

- You attract people who don't value you
- You experience rejection and abandonment
- Opportunities seem to pass you by
- Scarcity and struggle become common themes
- Relationships are characterized by conflict and dissatisfaction

GOD AS MIRROR: **How Self-Perception Shapes Reality**

"God is a mirror. It can only show you what you're giving off. That's all it can do." (Bashar)

This single truth is the foundation of all creation. If you look into a mirror and see a frown, it is not because the mirror is rejecting you; it is simply reflecting what you are presenting. If you wish to see a smile, you must smile first.

This applies not only to facial expressions but to your entire life.

• If you feel unworthy, reality reflects situations where you are ignored, rejected, or overlooked

• If you believe money is scarce, reality reflects financial hardship

• If you think love is hard to find, reality reflects people who are unavailable or unkind

The mirror does not judge; it does not care whether you smile or frown. It simply reflects what you project. This echo's the principle that life has no built in meaning. You have free-will and the power to choose how you will define your life and your reality. You have free will to decide, which frequency, you will vibrate on and thus what you will resonate with. It's all U.

SELF-LOVE: **The Starting Point for All Change**

If everything in your experience is a reflection of your internal state, then loving yourself is not just important—it is the foundational act of creation. Without self-love, you will constantly seek external validation, approval, and fulfillment, but the mirror can only give back what you are emitting.

This is why people who love themselves effortlessly attract love. It is why people who trust abundance effortlessly attract wealth. It is why people who radiate peace find peace everywhere they go.

Your relationship with yourself is the ONLY relationship you are ever having—because everything else is a reflection of that relationship.

UNDERSTANDING **HOW THE REFLECTION IS CREATED**

If the universe is a mirror, then we must understand what stands before it. What exactly is being reflected? How does the internal become external? How does the invisible become visible?

To truly work with the Law of Reflection, you must understand the architecture of creation itself: how your inner world constructs the outer world you experience. This is not philosophy. This is mechanics. This is the operating system of reality.

THE HOUSE BLUEPRINT

Consider a house. Every house begins not with walls or windows, but with a blueprint. Before a single nail is driven, before the foundation is poured, there exists an invisible design, a pattern that will determine everything that follows. The blueprint dictates the shape, the dimensions, the flow, the feel of the structure that will eventually stand.

Now consider the foundation. Once the blueprint is chosen, the foundation is laid. This is the base upon which everything rests. If the foundation is crooked, even slightly, the entire house inherits that distortion. Every wall built upon it will lean. Every door will stick. Every floor will slope. The crookedness doesn't stay contained at the bottom; it ripples upward through every level of the structure.

Here is what most people fail to understand: if the house feels cramped, unstable, or uncomfortable, repainting the walls will not fix it. Changing the curtains will not straighten what is crooked. Rearranging the furniture will not address what was built into the very bones of the structure.

You must return to the blueprint. You must examine the foundation.

This is precisely how your reality operates.

BELIEF/DEFINITION/PERCEPTION   =
Foundation/Blueprint

Your beliefs are the blueprint of your life. Your definitions, the meanings you assign to yourself, to others, to circumstances, to existence itself, are the foundation upon which everything else is constructed.

A belief is not merely a thought you think. It is a declaration of what is true for you. It is the invisible architecture that shapes what can and cannot exist in your experience. Before any emotion arises, before any thought forms, before any behavior manifests, there is the belief: silent, foundational, determining.

What do you believe about yourself? What do you believe about money? About relationships? About your worthiness? About what is possible for you? These are not idle questions. These are inquiries into the very blueprint from which your life is being constructed, moment by moment.

If your foundational belief is "I am not enough," then no matter what you build upon it, no matter how hard you work, how much you achieve, how many affirmations you speak, the structure will inherit that original distortion. The house will always feel unstable because instability was designed into its foundation.

This is why some people achieve external success yet feel perpetually empty. This is why others receive love yet cannot feel loved. The external construction may appear impressive, but the foundation was crooked from the start.

EMOTIONS = BUILDERS **Constructing the Inner World**

Your emotions are the builders. They are the workforce that takes the blueprint of your beliefs and begins constructing your inner reality. Emotions do not arise randomly. They are responses to the meanings you have assigned. They are builders following orders from the blueprint. You cannot have an emotion without first having a belief about that subject in your reality.

If your belief is "the world is dangerous," your emotional builders will construct an inner world of anxiety, vigilance, and fear. They are not malfunctioning. They are doing exactly what the blueprint demands. They are building according to plan.

If your belief is "I am loved and supported," your emotional builders construct an inner world of peace, openness, and trust. Same builders. Different blueprint. Completely different structure.

This is why you cannot simply "think positive" your way to transformation. Telling the builders to use brighter paint does not change the blueprint they are following. The emotions will continue constructing according to the foundational belief until the belief itself is changed.

When you feel persistent negative emotion, do not fight the builders. Thank them. They are showing you the blueprint. They are revealing what you truly believe at the foundational level. This is invaluable information. This is the feedback that allows you to return to the source and revise the design.

THOUGHTS = MATERIALS **Used in Construction**

Your thoughts are the materials the builders use. They are the wood, the stone, the glass, the steel of your inner construction. Every thought is a building material being selected and placed according to the emotional direction, which itself follows the belief blueprint.

Notice how thoughts cluster. When you believe something negative about yourself, thoughts of that same frequency appear, not randomly, but consistently. "I'm not good enough" attracts thoughts of past failures, future anxieties, comparisons to others. The builders are selecting materials that match the blueprint.

Conversely, when your foundation is solid, when you believe in your worthiness, your capability, your connection to Source, your thoughts reflect this. Solutions appear. Inspiration flows. Possibilities present themselves. The materials match the design.

This is why trying to control every thought is exhausting and ultimately futile. You are attempting to micromanage the materials while ignoring the blueprint that determines which materials are selected.

Change the foundation, and the thoughts shift naturally. The builders automatically reach for different materials because the design has changed.

BEHAVIORS = **How You Live Inside the Structure**

Your behaviors are how you live inside the structure you have built. They are the natural result of inhabiting the inner world your beliefs, emotions, and thoughts have constructed.

If your inner structure is built on fear, you will behave fearfully: avoiding, hiding, defending, attacking. These behaviors feel inevitable, automatic, because you are simply living in the house that was built. You cannot behave peacefully in a structure designed for war.

If your inner structure is built on love and trust, you will behave accordingly: opening, risking, giving, receiving. These behaviors flow naturally because they match the environment you inhabit internally.

This is why willpower alone rarely produces lasting change. You can force yourself to behave differently for a time, but you are still living in the same structure. The moment vigilance relaxes, you return to behaviors that match your inner architecture. You cannot indefinitely act against the environment you inhabit.

True behavioral change occurs when the inner structure changes. When the foundation shifts, when the blueprint is revised, when the builders construct something new, behavior transforms not through force, but through alignment. You simply begin living differently because you are now living in a different house.

EXPERIENCE = THE "HOUSE-LIFE" **You Inhabit**

Finally, your experience, the totality of what you perceive as your "life," is the house-life you inhabit. It is the culmination of all that came before: the blueprint chosen, the foundation laid, the builders at work, the materials selected, the behaviors that flow from living in that structure.

Your experience is not happening to you. Your experience is the inevitable result of the architecture you have created from the inside out.

This is both the confrontation and the liberation of this teaching. It confronts us because we can no longer blame external circumstances for our experience. The mirror reflects what we have built. But it liberates us because it means we have complete creative authority. We are not victims of a reality imposed upon us. We are architects who can revise the design.

RETURNING **to the Foundation**

Here is the practical application: when your life feels cramped, unstable, or persistently uncomfortable, stop trying to rearrange the furniture. Stop repainting the walls. Stop blaming the neighbors for how your house feels inside.

Return to the blueprint.

Ask yourself: What belief is this experience reflecting? What definition have I accepted as true? What foundational assumption is creating this distortion throughout my entire structure? Bashar often uses this question. "What would I have to believe is true about me with regard to this situation or event to be experiencing this?" A key to understand is that once you find out the belief and realize that it is nonsensical and no longer aligns with the truth of who you are, that is the end of the matter, not the beginning.

This is the work. This is the transformation. This is how you change the reflection, not by reaching into the mirror, but by changing what stands before it.

When you revise the blueprint, when you choose a new foundational belief about who you are, what you deserve, what is possible, everything built upon it must shift. The emotional builders receive new instructions. The thought-materials change to match. The behaviors align naturally. And the experience, your house-life, transforms from the inside out.

This is not positive thinking. This is reality architecture.

You are the designer. You are the foundation. You are both the house and the one who dwells within it.

Build accordingly.

APPLYING **the Mirror Principle to Every Aspect of Life**

Once you internalize that the outer world mirrors your inner state, you can see how this one principle applies to everything—health, wealth, love, purpose, and spiritual fulfillment.

1. Health: The Body Reflects the Mind

Your body is a mirror of your consciousness. Your thoughts, emotions, and beliefs directly influence your health and well-being.

• If you hold stress and fear, your body reflects this as tension, disease, and fatigue

• If you love and nurture yourself, your body reflects this as vitality, energy, and healing.

PEOPLE who constantly worry about illness tend to attract health problems. Those who believe in their body's ability to heal often experience remarkable recoveries.

Your body is not separate from your mind. It is a reflection of your definitions.

"As a man thinketh in his heart, so is he" (Proverbs 23:7, KJV).

2. Wealth: Abundance is a State of Being

Money is not something "out there" that you must chase. It is a frequency—a reflection of your relationship with yourself.

"You are always abundant. You are always trusting something.

You are always confident in something. The only question is: what are you trusting and being abundant in?" (Bashar)

If you believe money is hard to get, the mirror will reflect struggle. If you believe money is a natural part of life, the mirror will reflect flow.

THE APPLE TREE

Does the apple tree not produce the apple? Does the apple seed not produce the apple tree? The apple is not separate from the tree—it is the tree expressing itself in physical form. Within every seed lies the complete blueprint of the entire tree: its roots, branches, leaves, and capacity to bear fruit. But the seed contains even more—it carries the apple itself, the full cycle of creation encoded within its DNA, already written into its identity. The seed does not need to "earn" the right to become a tree; that right is inherent, woven into its very nature. It simply unfolds what it already is.

When the seed is planted in soil, the soil does not create the tree —it activates what is already encoded within the seed. The soil provides the environment for germination, the conditions for the seed to remember and express its true nature. In the same way, this third and fourth dimension reality is the soil of humankind. You were planted here not as a punishment, but as an activation. This physical dimension is the environment that triggers your germination—your awakening to what you have always been. The density of this reality creates the resistance, the pressure, the darkness necessary for you to push through and remember your divine blueprint.

In the same way, you are made in the image and likeness of God. You are not a diminished copy or a lesser version—you are a complete holographic expression of the Divine, containing within you the full blueprint of the Source. Just as the apple seed carries the entirety of the tree's potential and the fruit it will bear, you carry the entirety of God's attributes: creativity, abundance, power, wisdom, and infinite wealth. These are not gifts you must earn—they are your encoded birthright. You are not separate from God; you are God experiencing itself as your localized self in this dimension.

The apple does not question whether it contains the tree. It simply grows into what it already is. The seed does not beg the soil for permission to become a tree. Neither do you need permission to be your full authentic self.

This truth was declared from the very foundation of creation. In Genesis 1:26-27, the Divine spoke: "Let us make man in our image, after our likeness..." Notice the language: not "like our image" or "resembling our likeness," but IN our image—complete, whole, fully expressed. When God said "let US make man in OUR image," the Divine was declaring that you would be created AS god—a localized expression of the infinite, containing the full blueprint of Source within your being.

Jesus himself confirmed this truth when he declared in John 14:12: "Verily, verily, I say unto you, He that believeth on me, the works that I do shall he do also; and greater works than these shall he do." Read that again. Jesus—the one called Christ, the anointed one —explicitly stated that YOU would do the works he did, AND GREATER. Not "maybe" or "if you're lucky" or "if you're special enough." He said you SHALL do them. How is this possible? How can you perform the same works as Jesus, and even greater, unless you are imbued with the same Divine Knowing—the same "Christ Consciousness"—that he embodied?

Christ Consciousness is not exclusive to Jesus. It is the awakened state of remembering that you ARE the Divine in human form. Jesus was not the exception—he was the example. He came to show you what is possible when a human being fully remembers and operates from their true divine nature. When he said "greater works than these shall he do," he was not elevating himself above you—he was calling you UP to recognize the same power within yourself.

· · ·

THIS PRINCIPLE IS WOVEN throughout all of creation. Genesis 1:24 declares that every living creature reproduces "after its kind." Lions produce lions. Rabbits produce rabbits—never dogs, never eagles, always rabbits. Each species carries forward the exact nature, instinct, and essence of what it is. The offspring is not "less than" the parent. The lion cub is not a diminished version of its lineage—it IS lion, containing the full blueprint of what a lion is meant to be. This is the immutable law of creation: like produces like.

So when God creates humanity "in Our image and after Our likeness," what does God produce? God. Not a servant. Not a worshiper from a distance. Not a broken, fallen, separate being. God produces god. It is the fundamental law of the universe—each produces after its kind. The Divine does not break its own creative principle.

Yet somewhere along the way, humanity reversed this truth. Instead of recognizing that we are made in God's image, we began making God in OUR image. We took the infinite, all-knowing, all-powerful, ever-present Divine and squeezed it down to fit the limits of our imagination and understanding. We created a God who judges like we judge, who punishes like we punish, who withholds like we withhold. We made God small, distant, conditional—because we forgot we were vast, present, and unconditional. But this was never the intention of the Divine.

God did not create you small so you could spend your life begging to become big. God created you IN Its own image so you could REMEMBER you already are.

NOW LET'S ask ourselves a simple question. If I am made of God— if I literally am a fractal of God and I am "god" in my reality—if I am God experiencing itself as a localized self called me—how can I not possess all of the attributes of God, which include Wealth and Abundance? It's impossible not to be wealthy. You do not become abundant. You remember that you already are. To deny your abundance is to deny an aspect of who you truly are.

People who embody wealth consciousness do not operate from lack or desperation. They trust the universe as a mirror, knowing that their internal belief in abundance guarantees its external reflection.

The secret to wealth is not chasing money—it is aligning with the energy of abundance before it appears.

3. **Love: The Reflection of Your Self-Worth**

Love is not something you find—it is something you allow when you recognize that you already are it.

If you believe "I am unworthy of love," the mirror reflects people who abandon, mistreat, or reject you. If you believe "I am already love itself," the mirror reflects deep, meaningful, and harmonious relationships.

"Thus, you create reflections of other people to not give love to you, because you are not giving it to yourself." (Bashar)

This is why people who desperately chase love never find it, while those who radiate self-love attract it effortlessly. Love is not an external event—it is a reflection of your inner relationship with yourself.

BREAKING THE ILLUSION: **The Reality You Live Inside**

The biggest misunderstanding people have is that they are inside reality. In truth, reality is inside you.

"You are not in the universe. The universe is in you." (Bashar)

This means that your thoughts are not responding to reality—reality is responding to your thoughts. However, without clear understanding, you fall into the trap where your thoughts respond to your reality, allowing the outside world to dictate how you should feel. This is outside-in living. Now that you realize why this is unsustainable—as the fifth law states, "everything changes"—you can see how it will drive you insane. Life constantly changes around you. Chasing the trends, the TikToks, the Instagrams, or whatever the flavor of the month is, will keep you perpetually on the hamster wheel of life. Most people wait for the outside to change before they feel better. But the mirror can only reflect back what you are already projecting.

Stability comes from living from the inside out—from purpose, from passion, from understanding who you are and following your excitement. Living from the inside out not only gives you mental clarity and stability; it becomes your safe haven as the winds of life begin to toss people to and fro, those who remain locked into sensationalized news cycles and the chaos of the external world. Knowing who you are is the secret place spoken about in Psalm 91:

"He that dwelleth in the secret place of the most High shall abide under the shadow of the Almighty. I will say of the Lord, He is my refuge and my fortress: my God; in him will I trust" (Psalm 91:1-2, KJV).

The secret place is not a physical location—it is the inner sanctuary of your divine identity. It is the unshakable knowing of who you are beyond the shifting circumstances of the material world. When you dwell in this awareness, when you abide in the consciousness of your true nature as God experiencing itself, no external storm can displace you. The news cannot move you. The trends cannot define you. The chaos cannot penetrate the fortress of your inner knowing.

Yes, the winds will come.

THE PARABLE **of the Wise and Foolish Builders**

Matthew 7:24-27 (KJV):

"Therefore whosoever heareth these sayings of mine, and doeth them, I will liken him unto a wise man, which built his house upon a rock: And the rain descended, and the floods came, and the winds blew, and beat upon that house; and it fell not: for it was founded upon a rock. And every one that heareth these sayings of mine, and doeth them not, shall be likened unto a foolish man, which built his house upon the sand: And the rain descended, and the floods came, and the winds blew, and beat upon that house; and it fell: and great was the fall of it."

THE FINAL REALIZATION: **You Are Everything You Seek**

At the deepest level, you are not seeking anything external. You are seeking a version of yourself that has already become the thing you desire.

"The thing that we think we want is not what we want. We want what we think is on the other side of having it. And that experience is already in me." (Peter Crone)

Everything you want—love, success, wealth, health, freedom—is already inside you. The only thing standing in the way is the illusion that it is outside of you.

• You do not wait for success to feel successful—you become successful internally, and the mirror reflects it

• You do not wait for love to feel loved—you love yourself first, and the mirror reflects it

• You do not wait for abundance to feel abundant—you align with the vibration of abundance, and the mirror reflects it

THE EXCEPTION

There is a nuance to the mirror principle that must be understood, lest we fall into spiritual confusion or unnecessary self-condemnation.

When we speak of people as reflections, we do not always mean a one-to-one correspondence. The mirror of reality is far more sophisticated than a simple echo. Not every person who enters your life carries a trait you must claim as your own. Not every challenge presented to you is a direct indictment of your character.

Consider this: when someone enters your experience carrying a particular negative issue, perhaps anger, insecurity, or judgment, the immediate temptation is to assume you share this same issue. But this is not always the case. The mirror sometimes shows you not what you are, but what you are willing to do.

THE PRACTICE **of Honest Self-Examination**

Here is where your divine discernment becomes essential. When confronted with another's issue, the first step is always honest self-investigation. Ask yourself with genuine openness: Does this person carry something I need to understand about myself? Is there truth here that will help me grow, that will make me a more aligned, more whole being?

If the answer is yes, receive it. Let their presence be a gift that illuminates what was hidden within you. This is the mirror functioning in its purest form.

But here is the exception: if, after sincere self-examination, you recognize that this issue does not belong to you, that it is not a reflection of who you are or who you have been, then the reflection shifts meaning entirely.

THE REFLECTION **of Service**

When someone else's issue is not your issue, they have not appeared in your reality by accident. They are still your mirror. But what they now reflect is not a shared wound. They reflect your willingness to be of service. They reveal your capacity for compassion. They illuminate what you are willing to do to help another soul find their way.

This is the deeper teaching: the mirror does not only show you your shadows. It also shows you your light. It reveals not only where you need healing, but where you have healed enough to help another.

.   .   .

RELEASING **What Was Never Yours**

Many of the beliefs that cause us to accept every reflection as our personal issue were not truly ours to begin with. As children, we absorbed the fears, judgments, and limitations of those around us: parents, teachers, society. We could not yet distinguish between what belonged to us and what belonged to them. Every criticism felt true. Every negative projection found a home in our developing consciousness.

But as adults walking in divine knowing, we can now see clearly. We can examine the beliefs we carry and ask: Is this truly mine? Or is this something I inherited from those who raised me, from circumstances I had no power to understand at the time?

The fear-based beliefs, the patterns of unworthiness, the reflexive assumption that every conflict reveals your fault: many of these were never about you. They were about whoever was struggling in your presence when you were too young to know the difference.

THE SOVEREIGN CHOICE

Now you have the power to decide. You get to choose whether another's presentation is medicine for your soul or an invitation to serve theirs. You are not at the mercy of every reflection. You are the one who determines its meaning.

When the mirror shows you someone else's pain, and you know that pain is not your own, recognize the truth: They are in my life so that I might be a reflection of love for them. They are here so I can demonstrate what it looks like to help another find their way.

This is still reflection. But it is the reflection of your highest self, the part of you that came here not only to heal, but to help heal. Not only to receive, but to give.

The mirror never lies. But wisdom is required to interpret what it shows.

. . .

PERSONAL EXAMPLE: **Transforming Marriage Through the Mirror Principle**

Another example of how I've applied the Divine Knowing principles to overcome real-life challenges and transform difficult situations has come in the form of my marriage. Needless to say, after years of living for my son in a high-stress environment, my wife and I were burnt out. We had come through this birth injury; shortly afterwards, we had to file for bankruptcy; then the pandemic hit, and we were not in the greatest of places. Statistically speaking, parents with special-needs children are significantly more likely to divorce due to the stress of the situation. I can attest that this is true. I certainly didn't want to divorce—my wife was "my person"—but we didn't like ourselves or who we had become, much less one another.

There are many aspects of Divine Knowing that I utilized to bring myself into a better place. One of the most important was the understanding that my only real responsibility is to bring myself into alignment. You can't give what you don't have, and my responsibility first was to make sure that I was in alignment and plugged in. It's like the instructions you receive on an airplane: in case of an emergency, parents are to put their mask on first, then help their children or others. I had to put on my spiritual mask of alignment and get myself into a better place. I couldn't worry about others before that. So this became a routine, a ritual, a means of survival.

Daily, I began walking in the park. I would pray, recite my affirmations, and talk to God, really trying to get myself into a routine of alignment and into a better spiritual space—remembering who I am, who I was, and who I wanted to become. This helped tremendously.

During this time, Bashar began talking about the mirror concept. This basically means that when you look in the mirror, you don't reach into the mirror to fix your clothes or your hair. No, you realize that you are looking at a reflection, and you must fix yourself in order for the reflection to change. You must smile if you want the mirror to smile back. Also pivotal was the understanding that we live in an "inside-out" universe. The Bible says, "As a man thinketh, so is he" (Proverbs 23:7, KJV). These understandings were tremendous to my outlook on my wife and my marriage. They basically put the onus back on me to change, and not to go pointing the finger at my wife in any circumstance. I had to fix my own clothes first, as my outward reality was a reflection of my state of being. Change my state, and eventually my outward reality would change. So this is what I began to do.

I completely let my wife off the hook for being responsible for my happiness. My happiness, my alignment, was my first priority—and it was up to me. As Abraham says, "Alignment is not like a college degree—once you have it, you always will. It's a day-by-day choice." One of the five divine laws is "What you put out, you get back." We live in a reflective universe, so I needed to be the state that I wanted to experience. Beingness is practiced—it's not just trying something on; it's a commitment to yourself. I had to grow and become a better version of myself by choosing happiness daily. I had to choose to be in alignment with higher frequency thoughts. I had to choose to smile, I had to choose to appreciate even the small things. I completely let my wife off the hook, and I took responsibility for my own life, my own alignment, my own happiness. This saved our marriage.

It was not easy, but it was well worth it. Even more so, it is the work that I believe we truly sign up for when we choose to marry. Marriage is a covenant that we enter into with someone we are supposed to love. However, the true purpose of marriage is that the other person reflects back to us, in a close-up way, parts of ourselves that we must tend to. It is up to us to do the work in the mirror of fixing ourselves. Marriage is a soul contract that should make us better. The better comes from a willingness to "own our own shit," and as Michael Jackson famously said, "look at the man or woman in the mirror, and make a change."

. . .

CHAPTER 4 KEY TAKEAWAYS:

- Reality is a mirror that reflects your internal state back to you
- Self-love is the foundation for all positive change in your life
- You cannot change the reflection without first changing what's being reflected
- Everything you seek externally already exists within you

FIVE

CHAPTER 5: WORTHINESS - SELF-WORTH - HOW DO WE DERIVE OUR TRUE VALUE

The Foundation of All Creation

As a technical engineer, I understand that systems operate based on fundamental principles. If a structure lacks a solid foundation, it cannot hold weight. If a program is missing core logic, it cannot function correctly. The same principle applies to existence itself. If you do not understand your place in reality, everything else—your perception of success, love, abundance, health—becomes unstable.

So let's establish the groundwork for reality itself.

EXISTENCE IS INTENTIONAL: **You Were Created for a Reason**

The universe—All That Is—is a supreme intelligence—an infinitely expansive, self-aware consciousness. It does not create by accident. It does not make mistakes. It does not generate anything without purpose.

And yet—YOU exist.

This alone is the ultimate proof of your worthiness.

- If you were unnecessary, you wouldn't exist
- If you had no value, you wouldn't be here
- If you had no purpose, you would never have been created

"Without you, All That Is would not be All That Is." (Bashar)

This is not just philosophy—it is physics. The structure of existence itself dictates that everything within it has a role, or else it would not be. Your existence is the supreme validation of your worthiness. There is no test you need to pass. No approval you need to seek. No status you need to attain. If you exist, you matter.

The divine intelligence of the universe does not create anything meaningless. Therefore, you are not meaningless.

THE UNIQUE DESIGN OF YOU: **Your "Soul Print"**

Your worth is not generic—it is specific. You were not created as some interchangeable being. You were not mass-produced. You are a one-of-a-kind phenomenon.

Just as every fingerprint is unique, you carry something even more distinct—what I call your soul print: a spiritual framework for understanding your irreplaceable uniqueness. While this concept exists across many wisdom traditions under various names (some speak of "energetic signatures," others of "vibrational blueprints"), I offer it here not as scientifically proven fact, but as a coherent model for recognizing and honoring the multilayered pattern of your being.

Your soul print is your unique vibrational signature—a living pattern composed of consciousness, frequency, gifts, desires, and resonance. It reflects how you dream, feel, choose, breathe, and align. More than identity, it is a harmonic expression shaped by how you resonate within yourself and with the field around you.

Here are qualities that compose this framework—not as an exhaustive or empirically verified list, but as doorways for contemplation:

. . .

1. **Core Field Qualities**

These form the central axis of your soul's vibrational integrity:

• Your Consciousness – The awareness field that witnesses, remembers, and evolves.

• Your Frequency – The oscillatory pattern of your being; how you harmonize or dissonate with others.

• Your Internal Coherence – The alignment of thought, emotion, breath, and action. (formerly "Phase Coherence")

• Your Breath Pattern – The symmetry and rhythm of your inhale/exhale; a gateway to presence. (Some call it "Breath Geometry")

2. **Personal Signal Features**

These are the unique, expressive elements of your vibrational identity:

• Your DNA as Harmonic Antenna – Encodes both physical form and energetic resonance. (Some call this a 'Tuning Fork')

• Your Gifts – The energetic functions you stabilize or transmit.

• Your Desires – The directional impulses that shape your waveform trajectory.

• Your Dreams and Aspirations – Pre-causal templates inviting manifestation.

• Your Intentional Depth – The amplitude and reach of your will, projected across timelines.

• Your Observational Presence – How you fold consciousness into form through awareness.

3. **Symbolic and Geometric Layers**

These aspects reflect how your soul interfaces with form, meaning, and number:

• Your Perspective – The geometric lens of your awareness.

• Your Soul Geometry – The triangulation of perception, integration, and resonance.

• Your Harmonic Number Pattern – Your unique resonance within the sacred number field.

• Your Symbolic Resonance – How archetypes and symbols activate within your field.

4. **Collective Interface Fields**

These reflect your contribution to the broader harmonic environment:

• Your Harmonic Memory – Recurring vibrational patterns echoing across lifetimes or timelines.

• Your Field Fractal – How your micro-choices ripple into macro-resonance.

• Your Contribution to Planetary Coherence – What your presence stabilizes or amplifies within the collective coherence grid.

There is no one else in existence with your exact vibrational blueprint-soul print. No one can replace you. No one can live your purpose but you. This means that your presence in the universe is irreplaceable. If you were missing, something essential to the whole would be lost. You are a specific aspect of the divine that only you can express.

"You are not merely in the universe; the universe is within you." (Bashar)

When you truly accept this, you begin to see that you are not small, insignificant, or powerless. You are a direct extension of the creative force of the universe.

THE MIRROR OF SELF-WORTH: **Understanding Your Divine Value**

Now, let's take this foundational understanding and connect it to self-love and self-worth.

We established that the universe does not create without purpose —so if you exist, you are needed. The very fact of your existence is divine confirmation of your worth.

But many people struggle with self-worth because they look outside of themselves for validation.

• They seek approval from others
• They measure their worth based on external success
• They determine their value by whether or not they feel loved, admired, or accepted by someone else

But here's the truth:

The mirror of reality cannot show you something you do not first accept within yourself.

"God is a mirror. It can only show you what you are giving off." (Bashar)

"As a man thinketh in his heart, so is he" (Proverbs 23:7, KJV).

You do not wait for the mirror to change—you change first.

SELF-WORTH **as the Foundation of Abundance**

Bashar teaches that true abundance is inseparable from worthiness. The experience of abundance in all its forms—financial, relational, emotional, and spiritual—is a direct reflection of your level of self-worth. The fundamental misunderstanding many individuals hold is that worthiness is something that must be earned, proven, or validated externally. This belief is false. Your very existence is proof of your inherent worth. The fact that you are here means that creation has deemed you necessary. If you were not worthy, you would not exist, because creation does not make mistakes.

YOU ARE **a Drop of Creation Itself**

Bashar often uses the analogy of an ocean and its drops:

"If the entire ocean is divine, then every drop within it must also be divine. You are a drop of the infinite ocean of creation. You are made of the same intelligence, the same energy, the same essence as all that is."

This means that you are not separate from the divine—you are an expression of it. Since creation is infinitely abundant, and you are part of creation, you must also be abundant. The illusion of lack arises when you forget who you are.

When you identify with limitation, you create experiences of scarcity. When you remember your true nature, you naturally allow abundance to flow into your life.

THE MIRROR OF REALITY: **Worthiness Determines What You Receive**

Bashar explains that physical reality is a mirror. It does not give you anything—it simply reflects your beliefs, emotions, and energy state. If you believe you are unworthy, life will reflect lack and struggle. If you know your worth, life will mirror abundance and ease.

The mirror must change its reflection. This is not mystical—it is a universal law of vibration.

THE TRAP **of Seeking External Validation**

One of the most damaging misunderstandings about self-worth is the idea that it must be confirmed by others. Bashar warns that relying on external validation creates an endless cycle of neediness:

• When you seek worth from others, you place your power outside yourself

• No amount of external approval will ever be enough if you do not first validate yourself

• People who do not feel worthy often overcompensate by inflating their ego or demanding attention—yet still feel empty inside

True self-worth does not come from recognition, praise, or material success. It comes from the inner knowing that your existence is inherently valuable. "If you do not believe you are worthy, then no amount of external validation will convince you. If you do believe you are worthy, then no external rejection will make you doubt it."

THE PARADOX OF WORTHINESS: **You Don't Have to Prove It**

Worthiness is not something you earn. It is something you remember.

A key paradox is that the people who feel the need to prove their worth are the ones who doubt it the most.

Those who know they are worthy have nothing to prove.

• You are already enough

• You do not need to justify your existence

• You do not need to become someone else to be valuable

• You do not need permission to express your true self

When you let go of seeking validation and instead align with self-knowing, you shift into a state of effortless self-expression. And that is when abundance starts flowing.

PERSONAL EXAMPLE: FROM "LIGHT SWITCH" **Kid to Authentic Self**

Here's a personal example from my life of how I came to understand worthiness through challenging circumstances:

Growing up, my father was a bipolar, manic-depressive, alcoholic Vietnam veteran with PTSD. He was a farmer at some point, on a farm that produced very little money. He didn't get a chance to figure it out, and we were stuck to bear the brunt of the confusion. Needless to say, he controlled the mood of the household, and our mood depended on how he came home from the liquor house. Can I say home or hell hole? Hmm, not really sure. Anyway, on rare occasions he would come home in an okay-level mood, but often times he would come home very agitated and aggressive. Did I mention paranoid? Oh wow, sorry I didn't. He was also very paranoid that people were taking the nothing that he had. In the absence of any real enemies that were tangible, he turned that anger on his family.

Anyway, I say this all to say that our mood, posture, and disposition would immediately change to compensate for how he was. We didn't know if we were going to be playing the blinking game in the backyard while he pointed a 30/30 high-powered rifle, in our face, or if we were going to be taking a trip to the hospital because he decided we didn't do something he wanted us to. So we were always on high alert. As we got older, my brother and I started calling it the "light switch." This meant that we had the ability to adapt and change to whatever he came home with.

THE HIGHER PERSPECTIVE:

From the advantage of a spiritual perspective, he gave me so much content to work with. This is from the advantage of a spiritual perspective however. Being that hindsight is 20/20, as they say, this was not my perspective when I was going through it all. I didn't have any of these tools; I didn't know any of this. We were in survival mode for a decade, at least.

SOME OF THE AFTER EFFECTS:

The effects of living as a "light switch" kid, turning on and off multiple times a day, sometimes a week, caused me to develop a keen sense of reading my environment and living from the outside in. I learned how to adapt, to change, to become whatever I needed to become in the moment to survive—my jobs, my relationships, my friendships, my businesses. You get it. Well, as you can imagine, on the outside I looked very successful because I had adaptability as my friend. However, when you are living in a reality where one of the Universal Laws dictates that "What you put out you get back," it doesn't truly work that well. Why?

Because I didn't have me. I wasn't being authentic. I had no foundation from which to truly be myself.

COMING HOME:

This is another huge advantage that this understanding provided for me. It gave me myself back. I got to know who I was, what I was, where I was. I started to live from the inside out, not going into situations, reading them and adjusting myself, contorting myself with ten layers of masks to fit in and belong. Standing on one leg, being the clown for a group of people who didn't know who they were, much less care about who I was or what I had to deal with.

SIDE NOTE 1:

This is the very situation that many minorities face in corporate America. They have to become someone else, wear the mask, dance to the tune like a performing bear, in order to pay the rent, the mortgage, the car note. It leads to exhaustion and depression, because you are never allowed to express your authentic self for fear that you will be ridiculed—or worse, fired.

SIDE NOTE 2:

On a side note, this is the reason why many (not all) beautiful women struggle with mental health issues. Unless they are raised in a stable environment and have the opportunity to ground themselves in some type of understanding that allows them to "have themselves," they grow up surrounded by people who idolize them—people who put them on pedestals.

When you're constantly valued primarily for your physical appearance rather than your authentic self, you never develop a solid foundation of who you truly are beyond the surface. You become accustomed to people responding to your looks rather than your thoughts, dreams, character, or inner essence. This creates a disconnect between your external identity and your internal reality, leaving you vulnerable and without a true sense of self-worth that isn't dependent on others' approval or physical validation.

They live from the outside in—looking to others for validation of their worth, never anchored in their own internal knowing.

This is especially true when men want them physically, seeing them as objects rather than whole beings. Yes, it's the man's fault for objectifying; however, when you live with an outside-in paradigm, you have no control over who you are. You find yourself in situations created and controlled by someone else. This control often operates through money, but it can also manifest as physical dominance, abuse, or mental manipulation. I think you get my point.

Having yourself is one of the greatest gifts you receive from Divine Knowing. And as someone who once didn't have himself, I can attest firsthand that it is far better on this side.

This reminds me of an appropriate biblical verse that says the following:

Matthew 7:24-27 (KJV): "Therefore whosoever heareth these sayings of mine, and doeth them, I will liken him unto a wise man, which built his house upon a rock: And the rain descended, and the floods came, and the winds blew, and beat upon that house; and it fell not: for it was founded upon a rock. And every one that heareth these sayings of mine, and doeth them not, shall be likened unto a foolish man, which built his house upon the sand: And the rain descended, and the floods came, and the winds blew, and beat upon that house; and it fell: and great was the fall of it."

The house in this instance is not so much just Jesus, but it is the understanding of who you are, what you are, how you are. How this universe works. Divine Knowing represents this understanding for me. I hope it can help you as well.

CHAPTER 5 KEY TAKEAWAYS:

• Your existence itself is proof of your inherent worthiness and divine value

• You have a unique "soul print" that makes you irreplaceable in creation

• Self-worth must come from within before it can be reflected externally

• Worthiness is not earned—it is remembered and acknowledged

SIX

CHAPTER 6: THE HIGHER MIND VS. THE PHYSICAL MIND

Harmonizing with Divine Intelligence

Building upon the Five Laws of the Universe we established earlier, this chapter reveals how to harmonize with your Higher Mind to live in accordance with these divine principles. To comprehend the authentic nature of consciousness, we must first unlearn the concept that the body contains the soul. The reality is the reverse: your body exists within your soul. Your consciousness is not something confined within the physical form—it is an extension of something far greater.

Picture a round sphere of brilliant light—this symbolizes your true essence, your soul, your Higher Mind. Now, picture this sphere projecting a focused beam of energy toward a specific point within itself. That concentrated energy is you, your human expression, a crystallized aspect of a vastly greater being. Even while inhabiting a physical body, you never become disconnected from this expanded part of yourself. Your physical body is actually within your soul. You maintain constant connection to the Higher Mind, this oversoul, the divine intelligence that transcends time and space. Grasping this connection, and discovering how to harmonize with it, unlocks a life of effortless flow, power, and clarity.

THE HIGHER MIND—THE **Guide from the Mountaintop**

The Higher Mind , which is your Soul, operates like an eagle soaring above an expansive landscape. It observes the terrain, the routes, the barriers, and the infinite possibilities. It knows precisely where you are and how to direct you toward your highest potential. It communicates to you not through words, but through energy. Think Assassin's Creed for my gamers—the Higher Mind has that elevated perspective, seeing the entire map while you're navigating at ground level.

HOW THE HIGHER **Mind Communicates**

• Intuition – Instant knowing, without logical explanation

• Excitement – The energetic draw toward something aligned with your purpose

• Nudging & Promptings – Subtle signals guiding you in a particular direction

• Green Light Synchronicities – Meaningful coincidences that reveal hidden guidance

• Red Light Synchronicities—Constant obstacles that clearly indicate that this is not the way—currently.

Your Higher Mind, "your soul" never communicates through fear, doubt, or hesitation—those are the voices of the Physical Mind, shaped by conditioning. To trust the Higher Mind is to surrender—not in weakness, but in faith. As Bashar states, "Surrendering to the flow is not about losing control; it is about surrendering to the control that is already built in." Your Higher Mind already recognizes the path of least resistance to your greatest joy. The only question is: will you listen? Does this path mean, that it will be without obstacles? No, it doesn't, however even the obstacles encountered serve you in a positives sense if you use your power to "Frame your reality correctly" More on this later.

THE PHYSICAL MIND—THE **Limited Perspective**

The Physical Mind resembles a hiker navigating through a canyon. It can only perceive what lies immediately ahead, attempting to make choices based on logic, fear, and previous experiences rather than divine intelligence. The Physical Mind functions as a receiving device. It gathers information and analyzes it. An important distinction is to understand that the physical mind can only perceive based on the frequency, or the wavelength it is tuned into. The critical question is: What frequency are you tuned into?

LIMITATIONS **of the Physical Mind**

- It can only analyze what is immediately apparent
- It gets influenced by fear, doubt, and cultural conditioning
- It frequently selects safety and security over growth
- It often challenges the signals from the Higher Mind instead of accepting them

The role of the Physical Mind is not to guide or lead—it is to accept direction from the Higher Mind. When you depend exclusively on the Physical Mind, you live in reaction mode. When you synchronize with the Higher Mind, you live with intention, confidence, and flow. A whole person is one whose Physical Mind operates in harmony with their Higher Mind, accepting guidance and input.

HOW TO FOLLOW **the Guidance of Your Higher Mind**

Your Higher Mind understands the route, but it will not compel you to walk it. It directs through the route of minimal resistance, consistently revealing the immediate step, but never the entire journey. You can follow this direction by cultivating alignment.

PRACTICAL STEPS TO **Align with the Higher Mind**

1. Pause and Listen – When facing decisions, halt and sense. Does the idea generate excitement or hesitation? Your emotions expose alignment.

2. Follow the Pull of Excitement – Your genuine path consistently emerges through what energizes you.

3. Detach from Outcomes – Trust that the Higher Mind perceives beyond your current view. Release the urge to control results.

4. Shift Your Perspective – Rather than asking, "Why is this occurring to me?", inquire, "How does this serve my growth?"

5. Use Your Emotions as a Compass – The more positive you feel, the greater your alignment. If you feel disconnected, modify your thoughts.

The more you rely on the Higher Mind, the more synchronicities, possibilities, and miracles emerge. This is not magic—this is alignment.

HERE IS **Abraham on the Inner Being (Higher Mind)**

"Hear this—we've not said this to you before, but it's time for you to know this... Your Inner Being has a point of attraction too. And while your Inner Being cannot throw something to you, it can hold the knowing of what you're asking for in such clear awareness that your point of attraction becomes more vivid and more powerful because you have asked, do you get that?"

Your Inner Being (Higher Mind, or Soul) never doubts, never worries, and never contradicts itself. It maintains the vibrational awareness of your desires and draws you toward them. However, you can obstruct this alignment by:

• Concentrating on what's missing instead of what's available
• Entertaining thoughts that oppose what you have requested
• Watching current circumstances instead of trusting the wisdom of your Higher Mind

When you ask, it is provided. The question becomes: Are you accepting it, or are you blocking it with your attention on what hasn't yet manifested? You always have assistance. You always have direction. The question becomes simply, are you receptive to receiving it? What channel are you on? The News? Instagram? Twitter? Twitch? Your Boss? Religion? What captures your attention? What is your daily routine for staying receptive?

BASHAR **on the Higher Mind and Excitement**

Bashar explains that your Higher Mind communicates to you through excitement because excitement represents your authentic signature vibration. It functions as a compass, a guide, a calling toward your genuine path. The Physical Mind cannot know how everything will develop—that belongs to the Higher Mind.

HOW TO USE **the Higher Mind's Guidance**

• Trust the process – Do not demand how things should develop
• Act on your highest excitement – Take any step in alignment with excitement, no matter how small
• Follow the synchronicities – They are your Higher Mind coordinating the perfect path

"Your Higher Mind already knows the best possible way for you. Stop trying to override it with Physical Mind logic. It was never designed to lead, only to experience." (Bashar)

HERE ARE **my top 10 Comprehensive Ways to Tune Into Higher Vibrational Frequencies:**

1. Meditation Quieting the mental chatter to create space for divine alignment and inner stillness

2. Getting Out in Nature Immersing yourself in the natural frequencies of creation; earth, water, trees, and sky recalibrate your energy

3. AAA (Triple A Formula) Acknowledging, Appreciating what you have, and Allowing the divine to flow in

4. Journaling Writing to process, clarify, and dialogue with your Higher Mind; capturing downloads and releasing resistance

5. Conscious Breathwork Using intentional breathing patterns to shift your state, calm your nervous system, and open receptivity to divine guidance

6. Movement and Embodied Presence Dance, yoga, walking, or any practice that moves stagnant energy and reconnects you to the wisdom of your body

7. Acts of Service and Giving Contributing to others without expectation; shifting from lack-consciousness into abundance flow by affirming you have something valuable to offer

8. Deliberate Morning Intention-Setting Beginning each day by consciously choosing your vibrational frequency before the world dictates it to you; asking "What channel do I choose today?"

9. Creative Expression Painting, music, writing, cooking, building—any flow state activity that bypasses mental resistance and lets Source move through you

10. Limiting Vibrational Contaminants Consciously reducing exposure to fear-based media, toxic relationships, complaining, and environments that pull you into lower frequencies; protecting your energetic space

LIVING YOUR HIGHER MIND CONNECTION: **Practical Applications**

. . .

THE NECESSITY **of Physical Action**

Many people believe that spiritual alignment alone will transform their reality. However, divine guidance must be expressed through tangible steps to fully materialize. Your Higher Mind provides the inspiration, but your physical being must translate that guidance into concrete movement. Without this earthly expression, spiritual insights remain as unrealized potential. Taking action—even simple steps—bridges the gap between inner knowing and outer manifestation. Bashar often indicates that physical action is like grounding the circuit in physical reality. It is something that has to be done to bring heaven down to earth, or spirituality into the natural.

WALKING **as Your Future Self**

A transformative practice involves embodying the version of yourself you wish to become. Each day, as you move through your environment, ask yourself: How would my highest self navigate this moment? Would they carry themselves with greater confidence? Would their energy be lighter and more purposeful? Would they move with certainty rather than hesitation?

By physically adopting the behaviors and energy of your desired reality, you create an energetic bridge between where you are and where you're going. This isn't pretending—it's practicing the frequency of your future self until it becomes your natural state.

UNDERSTANDING **True Abundance**

Bashar defines abundance as "the ability to do what you need to do when you need to do it." This definition transforms our understanding of prosperity beyond mere financial accumulation. While money often symbolizes abundance in our culture, genuine prosperity flows through countless channels: opportunities, connections, knowledge, resources, and divine timing.

When you release rigid expectations about how support must arrive, you open yourself to receive assistance in forms you may never have considered. The universe operates through infinite pathways of provision, and your job is to remain flexible about which route your needs will be met.

THE ECHO PRINCIPLE

When you begin shifting internally, your external world often continues reflecting your previous patterns for a time—this is what we call "the echo." Old situations, familiar triggers, and past circumstances may still appear, but they serve a crucial purpose: they reveal whether you've truly transformed.

The test of genuine change isn't whether your circumstances immediately shift, but whether you respond to familiar challenges with a new consciousness. When you react differently to the same situation, you signal to reality that you've genuinely evolved, allowing your external world to eventually mirror this internal transformation.

LABELING REALITY

Every experience you encounter or you enter into arrives without inherent meaning—it becomes positive or negative only through the interpretation you assign to it. This connects to the deeper principle we'll explore in Chapter 9: reality serves as a neutral canvas waiting for your conscious definition.

The power lies in recognizing that you're constantly assigning meaning to events, and these assignments determine your energetic response. When you consciously choose empowering interpretations —viewing obstacles as redirections, delays as divine timing, challenges as growth opportunities—you transform the very fabric of your experience. Your consistent practice of positive labeling gradually shifts your entire reality to match this elevated perspective.

. . .

RELEASING **Disappointment**

Disappointment emerges when reality doesn't unfold according to our predetermined timeline or expectations. However, this emotional response reveals an underlying assumption that something has gone wrong when circumstances don't match our mental pictures.

True empowerment comes from recognizing that where you currently stand is precisely where you need to be for your highest growth. Rather than making your peace conditional on external outcomes, practice maintaining inner alignment regardless of temporary appearances. This doesn't mean becoming passive—it means trusting that divine timing orchestrates events more perfectly than your limited perspective could arrange.

NO WRONG CHOICES

From a Higher Mind perspective, there are no incorrect decisions —only different pathways that provide unique learning experiences. Every choice you make serves your evolution, even when the outcome differs from your expectations.

When a decision leads to unexpected results, resist labeling it as a mistake. Instead, recognize it as valuable information that clarifies your preferences and guides future choices. This perspective eliminates the paralysis that comes from fear of making wrong decisions. You can move forward confidently, knowing that every path contributes to your growth and understanding.

PLAYFULNESS AS MASTERY

True mastery reveals itself through a sense of lightness and play rather than struggle and strain. When you approach life with curiosity and flexibility instead of rigid seriousness, you become more responsive to the natural flow of opportunities and synchronicities.

Heaviness in your approach creates resistance in your experience, while a playful attitude allows circumstances to shift more easily. Joy naturally elevates your frequency, making you magnetic to positive outcomes. Fear creates density that slows manifestation, while lightheartedness accelerates the flow of desired experiences.

Cultivating an exploratory mindset—treating life as an adventure rather than a test—opens you to possibilities that serious, worried thinking cannot perceive.

CONCLUSION: **The Power of Divine Alignment**

The greatest secret of existence is not that you are separate from God, but that you are one with God.

Your Higher Mind is always guiding you. Your emotions reveal your state of alignment. Your thoughts and declarations shape your reality. When you fully embrace this truth, you will move beyond struggle, beyond fear, beyond limitation. You will no longer live as a passenger in life, but as a creator.

CHAPTER 6 KEY TAKEAWAYS:

• Your Higher Mind is your divine guidance system that sees the bigger picture

• The Physical Mind is meant to receive direction, not lead your life

• Excitement is your Higher Mind's way of showing you divine direction

• Follow your bliss—your excitement is divine guidance

• Physical action is required to ground this excitement into physical reality. You must act on the inspiration in the physical.

• Alignment with your Higher Mind creates effortless flow and synchronicity

• Responding differently to familiar situations proves the new state of being and creates new realities

- Playfulness and trust accelerate spiritual mastery and transformation

SEVEN

CHAPTER 7: USING THE TOOLS: THE PATH TO CONSCIOUS MANIFESTATION

It is essential to understand that the practical implementation of these tools is what anchors them into your physical experience. By taking form in a physical body, you have indicated your intention to participate in a process of self-discovery, to explore fresh perspectives of yourself through concrete experiences. Every action you take functions as a form of commitment, a declaration to creation that you are deliberately harmonizing with its principles. Simply maintaining these concepts in your mind is inadequate; transformation happens through lived experience. Below is my interpretation of a lecture by Bashar entitled 'Using the Tools.' This is by far one of his most profound lectures on using physical action to ground spiritual principles.

We have discussed extensively The Five Laws of Existence and The Formula of Acting on Your Highest Excitement. These principles function as the foundation of conscious manifestation:

THE FIVE LAWS **of Existence**

. . .

YOU EXIST – This indicates that if you exist presently, you eternally will. Though your form may alter, your essence stays eternal. If you were not vital to the wholeness of existence, you simply would not be. There are no errors in creation.

EVERYTHING IS HERE AND NOW – Time and space are illusions, frameworks that permit you to experience reality from a sequential perspective. In actuality, all realities exist simultaneously.

THE ONE IS THE ALL, **and the All is the One** – There is no authentic separation. Everything represents an aspect of the same boundless consciousness, experiencing itself through varied perspectives.

WHAT YOU PUT **Out is What You Get Back** – Physical reality serves as a perfect mirror of your inner state. Your beliefs, definitions, and vibrational frequency shape what you encounter.

EVERYTHING CHANGES, **Except the First Four Laws** – Change constitutes the core mechanism of expansion. Expansion and transformation remain the only constants.

THE FORMULA **for Acting on Your Highest Excitement - Bashar**

Equally crucial is The Formula for Acting on Your Highest Excitement, a three-step methodology for harmonizing with your authentic vibrational signature:

.   .   .

ACT **on whatever excites you most in any given moment.** Your excitement functions as a signal from your higher self, steering you toward alignment with your genuine path.

PURSUE **it as far as possible, to the best of your capability.** This does not involve forcing things but rather pursuing the organic progression of excitement until no further action remains.

RELEASE **all attachment to the outcome.** The Physical Mind lacks the design to foresee how events will develop; that belongs to the Higher Mind. Trust that the process itself is directing you precisely where you belong.

By implementing these principles, your life transforms into a seamless flow, a harmonious dance with the structure of creation. Resistance melts away, and synchronicity becomes the guiding force that positions you at the right place, at the right time, with the right people. Reality becomes effortless.

YOUR EXCITEMENT **as a Complete Kit**

Your excitement operates as a comprehensive toolkit, containing every instrument necessary for expansion. It functions as:

• The motivating force of your existence, powering your drive and mental clarity.

• The structuring principle that coordinates experiences in the most beneficial order.

• The route of minimal resistance, guaranteeing you consistently move with the organic flow of your energy.

• The linking thread, connecting apparently unrelated experiences into a unified journey.

• The revealing mirror, uncovering limiting beliefs so they may be acknowledged and transformed.

Everything in existence functions as a frequency-based system. Your beliefs and definitions establish your vibrational state, which subsequently determines what experiences reality reflects back to you. If you witness negativity in your life, it occurs because you are operating from a definition that creates that reflection. By identifying and transforming those limiting beliefs, you adjust the frequency you broadcast, thereby changing your experience.

Creation itself remains neutral; it does not judge. The mechanism of existence does not concern itself with what you choose—it simply mirrors your choice back to you. Whether you choose positivity or negativity, the universe responds, "Agreed" and reflects it accordingly.

Understanding this grants you absolute empowerment: You alone determine the meaning of your experiences.

MASTERING THE TOOLS: **Becoming the Architect of Your Reality**

MANY OF YOU search for techniques, approaches, and direction on how to manifest changes in your lives. But the fundamental understanding you must absorb is that you are already manifesting, every moment. The question is not whether you are creating—it is whether you are creating deliberately or unconsciously.

Physical reality functions as a mirror; it does not possess an inherent nature of its own. It is simply an externalized projection of your internal definitions and beliefs. If you gaze into a mirror and witness an unhappy expression, you do not attempt to alter the reflection first. You modify your expression, and the reflection follows. Similarly, changing external circumstances proves pointless unless you first transform the internal definitions that generate them.

Many of you grow discouraged when, after transforming your beliefs, you still encounter the same external circumstances. This happens because reality often delivers an "echo"—a persistent reflection of previous definitions. It is not a sign that you have failed to change; rather, it represents a chance to respond differently. The genuine measure of transformation is not whether circumstances shift immediately but whether your response to them has evolved.

WHEN YOU REACT **from a new state of being, reality must eventually align.**

THE MIND TENDS to resist change, grasping familiar narratives out of fear. But authentic mastery demands stepping beyond this fear and trusting in the alignment of your excitement. Remember: You do not require a reason to be happy, except that you prefer it. Conditional happiness, where joy relies on external validation, keeps you trapped in reactive cycles. Instead, select happiness as your foundational state, and observe as your reality reorganizes to mirror that choice.

Furthermore, manifestation is not about drawing something to you; it is about becoming the vibrational match to what you desire. When you embody the frequency of abundance, love, or success, those experiences naturally gravitate toward you. This is not magic—it is physics.

THE TRUE NATURE OF PRAYER: **Alignment, Not Petition**

Most people approach prayer as begging—a desperate plea from a place of emptiness: "Please, God, give me what I don't have." I understand completely; it is the way we were taught. But this approach contains a fundamental misunderstanding. It assumes you are separate from what you seek. It assumes provision is conditional. It assumes you must convince the Divine to give you something it's withholding.

This is prayer from lack. And lack cannot tune into abundance.

Prayer is not about asking for what's missing. Prayer is about aligning with what's already present.

THE SHIFT: **From Pleading to Presence**

The Divine is not a vending machine that dispenses blessings when you beg hard enough. The universe is not withholding from you. You are standing in an infinite field of possibility, love, and provision—right now. The question is not whether it exists. The question is: Are you tuned to the frequency where you can recognize and receive it?

True prayer repositions your consciousness. It doesn't change God's mind—it changes your receptivity.

GRATITUDE & **Appreciation: The Frequency of Reception**

IF ALL THE mystics are correct—Neville Goddard, who teaches you must assume the feeling of the wish fulfilled; the Bible, which states "Therefore I say unto you, What things soever ye desire, when ye pray, believe that ye receive them, and ye shall have them" (Mark 11:24)—then begging for anything, really asking for anything, is not the way you pray.

When you pray from gratitude, something profound happens. You stop broadcasting the signal of "I don't have." You begin resonating with "I am already held. I am already loved. I am already provided for."

Gratitude is the vibrational key that unlocks what already exists.

Notice the scripture doesn't say will receive—it says have received. Present tense. Already done.

When you pray with thanksgiving, you are not pretending. You are acknowledging the truth of the invisible reality before it becomes visible. You are aligning your frequency with the answer before your eyes can see it. Prayer is not a request for what you don't have. Prayer is a recognition of what you've already been given—resonating with the frequency of what is already yours.

MANIFESTATION IS RECOGNITION, **Not Acquisition**

MANIFESTATION DOESN'T MEAN something that didn't exist suddenly appears. It means you finally become receptive to what was always there.

Think of it like tuning a radio. The song was always playing—you just had to find the right station to hear it.

The field is always giving. Love is always flowing. Support is always present. What changes is not the availability—it's your ability to see it, feel it, and receive it.

The delay between prayer and manifestation is simply the time it takes for your inner state to stabilize in the frequency of what you're asking for. Change your internal resonance, and the external reflection must follow.

YOU ARE ALWAYS BEING GIVEN

THIS IS the foundation that changes everything:

You are not in a universe of scarcity, rationing, or divine favoritism.

You are in a field of infinite love, perpetual provision, and constant support. It does not turn on and off. It does not judge you as worthy or unworthy. It is always present—like oxygen, like gravity, like light.

You are always being:
- Loved
- Supported
- Provided for

What fluctuates is not God's willingness to give. What fluctuates is your willingness to receive.

If you don't feel supported or provided for, it's not because the love isn't there—it's because you're not yet in the vibrational state to perceive or experience it. This is not a punishment—it's simply how energy and perception work.

UNDERSTANDING FREQUENCY: **The Channel Analogy**

LET me provide better context to understand prayer in a practical way. Life operates like a cable system with thousands of different channels—each representing a different frequency.

Let's say you are currently operating on Channel 2.

What determines your channel? Your beliefs, which translate into your emotions, which translate into your thoughts, which translate into your words, which translate into your actions. These determine your set point—your state of being, your vibrational frequency. This frequency is always a mixture of who you are and who you are becoming.

Now let's say what you want is on Channel 60.

Channel 60 isn't just a number—it represents a completely different frequency. As a note of clarity: cable stations actually do tune by frequency behind the scenes. The different channel numbers represent different frequencies.

So the question becomes: How do you receive Channel 60 experiences when you're tuned to Channel 2?

The divine law says:
- "What you put out, you get back," right?

• "As a man thinketh in his heart, so is he" (Proverbs 23:7)

• "Seek ye first the Kingdom of God, and all these things shall be added unto you" (Matthew 6:33)

• "Believe that ye receive them, and ye shall have them" (Mark 11:24)

The answer: You must first tune yourself to Channel 60's frequency.

THE PROCESS: **Becoming the Frequency**

FIRST, you must use your imagination to feel what Channel 60 feels like. What would it feel like to have the thing you dream of? What does it look like? What does it feel like? More than just Channel 60 stuff is the understanding of not thinking of it but thinking from it.

Critical understanding:

You're not imagining the object—you're embodying the feeling it represents. The new car isn't what you truly desire; it's the feeling of accomplishment, success, and freedom that comes with it. You're not imagining winning the lottery; you're feeling what it's like to already be wealthy and abundant.

What does it feel like after years of having wealth? After all the shopping sprees, after the money you've blown or given away—who are you now? What does this person feel like once you've settled in beyond all the external stuff?

Not the moment of winning, but the settled feeling months or years later when wealth has become your natural state.

You're imagining the quiet moments after the blessing has integrated into your life. You're thinking of the moment when you've been married for a few years and you're sitting on the couch with your spouse, Netflix and chilling, cuddled under the blanket. You say to yourself, "God, thank you for looking out for me. You did your Big

1 with this blessing. I appreciate you for this." You're feeling the feeling of appreciation because it's already done.

This is what Neville Goddard calls "living in the wish fulfilled"—not a state of constant ecstasy or the peak excitement of first receiving, but something far more profound: the quiet certainty of already having. It's the gentle plateau after the mountain top, where relief meets release, where knowing replaces hoping. This is the natural state that emerges months after receiving your blessing, when novelty has transformed into a peaceful, unshakeable knowing.

This knowing is embodied, not merely mental. It transcends positive thinking or mind control attempting to override doubt. It becomes a conviction felt throughout your entire being—a complete mind-body resonance where everything in you vibrates with the truth of your fulfilled desire. Your body believes it. Your nervous system reflects it. No strain, no grasping, no performance—only relaxed, peaceful certainty. This is Neville's "feeling is the secret": not excitement, but settledness; not hoping, but knowing.

From this place, creation flows effortlessly. In this state, you truly live. It's a quiet, gentle space of relaxed certainty where imagination becomes dynamic, anchored not just in mind but in the deep conviction of your entire being. When mind and body align in this knowing, manifestation becomes as natural as breathing.

Peter Crone magnificently said that the thing we think we want is not really what we want. You say you want a new car or house, but what you really want is the sense of accomplishment or success that having these things would give you. As humans, we often make our happiness conditional: "Once I get this, then I'll be happy."

This mindset places our true goal—happiness—outside our grasp, always conditional on something else. We make our worthiness as women conditional on a husband and children. We make our worthiness as men conditional on approval from women or our social circle.

Living from the inside out allows you to go there in your mind and be "happy now." As many great sages have said, "Happiness is the way." The journey is the destination. The process is the point.

So how do you get what's on Channel 60 when you're on Channel 2?

Channel 60 must become your resonant frequency. What does the you on Channel 60 do daily? What are their habits? Their mindset? How do they approach life?

You might say, "If I had that stuff, I would be that person." I totally understand, but the truth of Universal law is that "Believing is Seeing"—not the other way around. You have to "BE" first before you "SEE" the reflection in your reality.

Now you understand why the journey is the destination—because it's who you become along the way of these transformations that is life. This is the journey you signed up to discover: more of yourself, more of the remembering of how this works, more of the unfolding of who you truly are.

HOW TO PRAY **from Divine Knowing: Practical Steps**

A SPIRITUALLY MATURE being doesn't ask for approval, worthiness, or abundance. Instead, they:
- Assume it's already granted
- Stand in the energy of already having
- Act and feel in gratitude for what is already true on a soul level

Correct prayer doesn't begin with "Please," but with "Thank you."

Not from desperation, but from trust. Not to convince God, but to align yourself. Not to acquire what's missing, but to attune to what's already here.

EXAMPLE:

✖ "God, please give me financial breakthrough. I'm so broke. I need help." (This prays from lack and amplifies the frequency of "I don't have.")

☑️ "Thank you for the provision that is already flowing toward me. Thank you for opening my eyes to see the opportunities around me. Thank you for the wisdom to steward what I'm being given." (This prays from alignment and opens receptivity.).

THE PRACTICE **of Appreciation**

The wisest course of action is to begin to appreciate Channel 2—here and now. What do you see around you that you can appreciate? Not much yet? I understand, but that is the key.

I personally ask my angels, guides, higher self, and Source for the "sight and understanding" to see more things in the here and now to appreciate. Here and now. At this moment. In this moment.

As you appreciate the here and now, you are in the highest frequency. It's easy to bridge to any timeline, any other channel through appreciation.

Daily I go to the park, and when I'm walking, I'm appreciating the here and now. My feet, my job, my wife, my kids—all things I can think of. Often, I go from A to Z, and on each letter I think of a new thing to appreciate about my life with that letter. By the time I'm finished, I can easily feel Channel 60 experiences, and I include those as well. It's natural. It's flowing. It's not forced. It's mine. Then I release it. If ever I think about it again, I just appreciate it more.

Appreciation is always a great state of being to be in.

CONCLUSION: **Shift from Asking to Knowing**

• Stop begging. Start aligning.

• Don't pray from lack. Pray from gratitude.

• Don't try to earn divine love or support. Realize you're already embraced by it.

• True manifestation happens not when something is finally given to you—but when you finally recognize it was there all along.

When prayer is understood and practiced as conscious alignment rather than desperate asking, it becomes one of the most powerful tools for maintaining the high-frequency states that attract miraculous manifestations.

Prayer from Divine Knowing doesn't beg.

It tunes in. It remembers. It receives.

I'll end this with a quote from Abraham Hicks:

"It is our promise to you: if you write things you appreciate in others, in life, and in yourself, you will have such a dramatic change in 30 days; and if you continued for 6 months, the change will be so powerful, so strong, that others who know you will not recognize the old you." —Abraham

CHAPTER 7 KEY TAKEAWAYS:

• The Five Laws and Formula for Excitement are your foundational tools for conscious creation

• Your excitement is a complete guidance system containing everything you need

• Reality is a frequency-based system that mirrors your internal state

• You are always manifesting - the question is whether it's conscious or unconscious

• Prayer is not about asking for what you lack, but acknowledging what you already have

• True prayer aligns you vibrationally with divine provision and support

EIGHT

CHAPTER 8: THE AAA FORMULA: ACKNOWLEDGE, APPRECIATE, ALLOW

Maintaining Alignment with Your Desired State.

The AAA Formula coined by Bashar is a practical tool for maintaining alignment with your desired state of being, especially when external circumstances appear to contradict your intentions. This formula helps you stay in a high-frequency state regardless of what is happening around you. Let me explain how it works below.

A - ACKNOWLEDGE: **Recognize What Is Already Present**

The first step is to acknowledge what you already have, rather than focusing on what appears to be missing. This shifts your attention from lack to abundance.

- Acknowledge your talents, resources, and opportunities
- Acknowledge the progress you have already made
- Acknowledge the support systems already in place

EXAMPLE:
- Instead of saying "I don't have enough money," acknowledge "I

have the ability to earn, create, and attract resources" Acknowledge whatever resources you do have.

A - APPRECIATE: **Express Gratitude for What Exists**

Appreciation is one of the highest vibrational states you can maintain. When you appreciate what you have, you signal to the universe that you are ready to receive more.
- Appreciate the small things as much as the large ones
- Appreciate challenges as opportunities for growth
- Appreciate the process, not just the outcomes

EXAMPLE:
- Instead of complaining about your current job, appreciate the skills it has taught you and the income it provides while you transition to something better

A - ALLOW: **Trust the Process and Release Control**

Allowing means trusting that the universe is orchestrating events in your favor, even when you cannot see the bigger picture.
- Allow solutions to come in unexpected ways
- Allow people to show up who can help you
- Allow timing to unfold naturally

EXAMPLE:
- Instead of worrying about "when" something will happen, allow the process to unfold naturally

HOW AAA HELPS MAINTAIN **the Desired State**

By acknowledging, appreciating, and allowing, you remain in a high-frequency state.

• This high-frequency state naturally attracts circumstances that match its vibration (Law of Reflection)

• When external reality still reflects old patterns, AAA helps prevent regression into old states of doubt, fear, and lack

CORRELATION BETWEEN THE AAA FORMULA **& The Fourth Law**

WHAT YOU PUT **Out is What You Get Back**

Bashar's Fourth Law states that your external world is a direct reflection of your internal state.

• If you vibrate at gratitude, joy, and appreciation, the universe must reflect circumstances that match that vibration

• If you vibrate at lack, frustration, and resistance, reality must mirror more of that lack

HOW AAA ALIGNS **with the Fourth Law**

Acknowledge → Aligns your awareness with what you already have, reinforcing an energy of abundance rather than scarcity

Appreciate → Puts out the frequency of gratitude, which attracts more to be grateful for

Allow → Ensures that you remain in the flow rather than forcing or resisting, which keeps you in alignment with your higher self

Together, this formula ensures that what you put out remains aligned with the reflection you prefer to receive.

PRACTICAL APPLICATION OF THE FORMULA **& the Fourth Law**

. . .

STEP 1: **Identify Your Desired State of Being**

Ask yourself: "What state do I want to embody?"

• Example: Abundance, peace, confidence, love, success, etc.

STEP 2: **Act As If That State is Already True**

Live as if you already embody that state.

• Respond to external "echoes" from the perspective of your new reality

EXAMPLE:

If you desire abundance, but an old bill arrives, do not react with fear.

INITIAL RESPONSE (STARTING POINT):

• Instead, acknowledge: "I always have what I need, and solutions always come"

• Understand: This is not going to be an immediate miracle change

• I once said, 'Thank you for having a 'Peter to rob to pay Paul"

THE TRANSITION:

This will be a practiced change; however, one day you will say:

EVOLVED RESPONSE (YOUR NEW STATE):

• Thank you, bills, because you are reflecting to me, validating that I have the ability to pay

• Thank you for the high-interest credit cards. They are serving me and will serve me

   • I appreciate the ability to have a "high-interest" credit card

   • I appreciate the opportunity to pay off my "high-interest" credit card

   • I appreciate my new credit cards that reflect my true worthiness

RESULT:

This solidifies the new frequency, eventually reflecting abundance externally.

STEP 3: **Use the AAA Formula to Maintain Your State**

   • **Acknowledge**: "I already have resources, talents, and opportunities"

   • **Appreciate**: "I am grateful for everything I currently have"

   • **Allow**: "I trust that abundance flows to me in perfect timing"

CHAPTER 8 KEY TAKEAWAYS:

   • The AAA Formula helps you maintain high-frequency states regardless of external circumstances

   • Acknowledge what you have, appreciate everything, and allow the process to unfold

   • This formula aligns perfectly with the Fourth Law: What you put out is what you get back

   • Consistent practice of AAA transforms your vibrational state and attracts matching experiences

NINE
CHAPTER 9: THE POWER OF MEANING: HOW YOU DEFINE REALITY CREATES REALITY

Life Has No Built-In Meaning -You Define It -Bashar

The foundational principle of existence is that life itself is neutral. It comes with no inherent meaning, no predetermined purpose. Reality is an empty canvas, a blank stage filled with neutral props, waiting for you—the creator—to define it.

Everything you experience is given meaning only through your perception and definition. "The greatest gift all of you have ever been given is that life is meaningless. You are designed to give life meaning. The meaning you give to every situation, positive or negative, determines how you experience the effect of that situation in your life." —Bashar

This understanding is not just an abstract concept—it is a direct key to self-empowerment. Since reality has no intrinsic meaning, you are free to assign meanings that serve you, that uplift you, that move you into alignment with the highest expression of yourself. What you put out is what you get back, meaning the way you define reality is how reality will be experienced.

. . .

WHAT YOU PUT **Out is What You Get Back**

This principle aligns directly with the 4th Law of Existence, which states: "What you put out is what you get back." This is not simply a philosophical idea—it is a fundamental, inescapable law of reality. Your frequency, your vibration, is shaped by the meaning you assign to events. The energy you radiate in response to an event is what determines the effect it has on you.

Every situation is neutral until you define it. If you define something as a curse, it will manifest as a curse—appearing in your reality in negative ways. If you define that exact same situation as a blessing, it will become a blessing.

What does this mean? It means that you are the divine force in your reality "god". You determine what effect something will have on you. What you put out is what you get back.

Even if someone intends harm upon you with their actions, if you remain neutral and declare, "I don't know why they did that, but it has to serve me in a good way," and you hold this stance as your mantra, that situation has no choice but to serve you positively. At the same time, the harm they intended will reflect back to them as the reciprocal of their actions.

Your neutrality becomes your shield. Your expectation of good becomes your compass. And the universe will and must honor both.

"If you define something negatively, you will get a negative effect. If you define the very same thing positively, you will get a positive effect. That's how it works. What you put out is what you get back." At the very least when calamity occurs go neutral, and have no opinion. Don't fall into the trap of programming that society as a whole has about situations and life.

ROMANS 8:28 **(KJV):**

"And we know that all things work together for good to them that love God, to them who are the called according to his purpose."

By choosing to assign a positive meaning to everything that happens in your life, you are literally using the power of creation properly. You are wielding your spiritual creative force in the way it was designed—to construct a reality that serves you, rather than one that limits you.

THE POWER **of Assigning Positive Meaning**

Since everything is neutral, and you define your experience, the highest form of personal mastery is the ability to consistently assign empowering meanings to all situations. This is not a game of delusion —it is the realization of your power as a conscious creator.

For example:

• A job loss can be seen as failure, or as an opportunity to transition into a more fulfilling career.

• A breakup can be perceived as a devastating loss, or as a necessary redirection toward self-discovery and better relationships.

• An unexpected obstacle can be labeled as misfortune, or as a stepping stone to something greater.

"Whatever it is that's coming to you is exactly perfect for what it is. Use it. Stay in the positive state and use it. It wouldn't be there if there wasn't a reason for it. You need to trust the way reality works. You need to trust the mechanism. You need to trust the structure."- Bashar

This is not blind optimism—it is the proper application of your spiritual creative power. By defining all things as serving you, you place yourself in alignment with reality's natural mechanisms, allowing you to receive the highest possible benefits from every situation. By maintaining a state of empowerment, you tune in to what "Source" is saying about you, so you are holding the frequency of the truth of yourself. This is power.

. . .

WHY ASSIGNING POSITIVE MEANING WORKS—THE **Science of Vibration**

When you positively define an event, you shift into a higher frequency state. This allows you to perceive opportunities, receive guidance from your higher mind, and navigate situations more smoothly.

If you define something as negative, you lower your vibration and block yourself from seeing the pathways where that very event could have led to expansion and empowerment.

"You cannot perceive what you are not the vibration of. Only by saying, 'I don't know why this happened, but I know it must serve me positively,' will you put yourself in the vibrational state to actually see how it is serving you." It may not be immediate. But hold the vibration and the reflection will come.

This is why it is so crucial to catch yourself in the act of defining things negatively and consciously reframe your perspective.

TRUSTING REALITY—THE **Ultimate Power**

When you truly trust that reality is always serving you, you step into absolute power. No matter what happens, you are unshakable because you already know that it must benefit you in some way. Life is not happening TO YOU, it is happening FOR YOU.

"If you know that no matter what happens, it's always going to benefit you, what do you care what happens? That's power. That's power. It doesn't matter what happens. It doesn't matter how things look. It doesn't matter what doesn't happen. It will always benefit me. That's power. That's a position of power. That's self-empowerment. Stay there. Don't leave it. Unless, of course, you like to suffer." – Bashar.

When you operate from this level of trust:

• Nothing in life can shake you. You recognize that even challenges are orchestrations for your growth.

• You radiate a frequency of stability and clarity. This attracts synchronicities, solutions, and harmonious manifestations.

• You stop resisting life and begin using it. Every event becomes a tool for self-mastery and expansion.

THE FORMULA **for Mastering Reality**

1. Recognize that all situations are neutral. They have no built-in meaning.

2. Catch yourself in the act of assigning meaning. Observe your initial interpretation.

3. Ask yourself if the meaning you assigned serves you. Does it empower you or disempower you?

4. Choose to assign a meaning that benefits you. Redefine the situation in a way that aligns with your highest good.

5. Maintain trust. Know that even if you do not understand how, every event has the potential to serve you positively.

PERSONAL   EXAMPLE: **Transforming   Life-Altering Challenges**

LET me share a clear example where I had to personally use this method. I worked for a manager with whom I had a good rapport. On my reviews, I typically received "meets expectations" or higher. During this particular review cycle, I got my standard "meets expectations" rating and my three percent cost-of-living raise. Everything seemed normal. Then, out of the blue, my manager called me. He was in tears. He told me that the VP of the company had personally contacted him and demanded that he change my rating to "did not meet expectations."

This was huge for me, as you can imagine. I had a new mortgage, a family, and my son is autistic—we depend on my job and insurance for his services. My manager said he would change my rating the following day and that I would be placed on a PIP (Performance Improvement Plan).

THE CONTEXT

At the time, my company was in the middle of some major personnel changes that were way above my pay grade. I honestly didn't know what to make of it all. I knew I couldn't tell my wife—she was in the midst of her own battle dealing with everything related to our son's needs.

I had known my manager from a previous job, and although I wasn't getting what the other employees were getting, I didn't think he would be racially motivated. However, I knew the company was letting people go, so maybe this was his way of doing it. I had never heard of a VP directly calling a manager to do such a thing, but I'm not in management, so I didn't know that either.

Either way, it was what it was, and I was behind the eight-ball.

WHAT I DID

So I did what I'm speaking about here. I first decided to go neutral. I couldn't see how it was going to serve me, but this was a lesson I had recently come across about a month or two before.

I didn't tell anyone. Not my mother, my brother, my wife, or my friends. No one.

I did exactly what I'm telling you here.

MY MANTRA

This became my mantra:

"I don't know why this is happening, but it's going to serve me in a good way."

I may have even said a few times: "I don't know why the HELL this is going on, but it's going to serve me in a good way."

DAILY PRACTICE

This became my daily mantra. Every morning, I went to the park and repeated it. I kept doing my job the best I could. I kept being positive. I did my best to only define things positively and speak life over myself.

New home. New mortgage. Kids in a new school. We finally thought we were moving up, and this hit. Wow.

"I don't know why this is happening, but it's going to serve me in a good way. I don't know why in the HELL this is happening, BUT it's going to serve me in a positive way!"

I didn't just say it. I made myself believe it. I began to give thanks for whatever was coming my way. It must be good!

PREPARATION

I knew that being placed on a PIP (Performance Improvement Plan) meant I needed to look for a new job. Often, PIPs are impossible to fulfill and are simply a means to properly exit you from a company. So I prepared my resume, joined LinkedIn Premium, and began my job search.

THE NEW JOB

Not long after joining LinkedIn Premium, I was contacted by a recruiter. After five interviews, I was hired with over $20,000 more in salary than my previous position—finally in line with the rest of my peers.

So not only did I get a better job—I got a better salary, with better benefits, with a better company!

. . .

THE AFTERMATH

I actually never told anyone that story until about a year later when my wife went through the exact same thing. Her boss flipped on her out of the blue after she'd received all these positive accolades, and she was placed on a PIP. I told her my story at that time, and we witnessed the Universe show up for her in the same way He did for me!

Won't He do it! God is the Dopest!

This is the power of defining reality from a place of trust rather than fear. The situation was neutral—the meaning I assigned transformed it into a blessing.

CONCLUSION: **Becoming the Creator of Your Reality**

The idea that life has no built-in meaning is not a statement of nihilism—it is a profound invitation to empowerment. It means that you are free to shape your experience in whatever way aligns with your highest joy, purpose, and evolution.

The true art of conscious living is the ability to assign meanings that uplift, expand, and transform every experience into an opportunity for growth and alignment. By mastering this principle, you shift from being a passive experiencer of life to an active creator of a meaningful, fulfilling existence.

"The situation has no built-in meaning. It is a prop. You give it meaning. The meaning you give it determines the effect you get out of it."

CHAPTER 9 KEY TAKEAWAYS:

• Every situation is neutral until you assign meaning to it

• The meaning you choose determines your experience and outcomes

• You have the power to redefine any circumstance in an empowering way

• Challenging situations are opportunities for spiritual growth and mastery

• When you assign positive meaning, you transform obstacles into stepping stones

TEN
CHAPTER 10: ABUNDANCE

The Reflective Reality of Abundance: Aligning with Your Natural Worthiness

Bashar defines abundance as "the ability to do what you need to do when you need to do it." This definition moves beyond the traditional notion that abundance is solely about money or material possessions. True abundance is a state of being where you trust that the universe will provide whatever is necessary for your highest good, in whatever form serves you best. Whatever! It doesn't always have to be money. Abundance is not something you acquire—it is something you allow. It's something that you are. It is your natural state, but it can be blocked by beliefs of unworthiness, scarcity, or the insistence that abundance must manifest in specific ways.

Not having positive abundance is a sign that there is something wrong. The good part about it is that as you re-connect to the truth of who you are you will begin to find your abundance in all ways, and that abundance will begin to appreciate, and appreciate, and appreciate.

· · ·

THE MIRROR PRINCIPLE **and Abundance**

Since reality is a mirror, your experience of abundance directly reflects your internal relationship with worthiness and trust. If you believe you are unworthy of abundance, or if you operate from fear and scarcity, the mirror will reflect experiences of lack. If you align with the knowing that you are inherently worthy and that the universe is abundant, your external reality will reflect prosperity in all its forms.

"You are always abundant. You are always trusting something. You are always confident in something. The only question is: what are you trusting and being abundant in?" (Bashar - Abundance)

Many people are abundant in worry, abundant in fear, or abundant in doubt. The key is to redirect that same energy toward trust, joy, and positive expectation.

BREAKING **the Illusion of Scarcity**

Scarcity is an illusion created by the physical mind's limited perspective. The universe is infinitely abundant—there is no shortage of energy, creativity, love, or resources. Scarcity only appears when you focus on what seems to be missing rather than recognizing what is already present.

The shift from scarcity to abundance happens when you:

• Recognize that abundance is already flowing into your life in countless ways

• Appreciate what you currently have, no matter how small it may seem

• Allow abundance by removing blocks and resistance (such as negative beliefs about money or worthiness)

• Trust that the universe will provide what you need, when you need it, in the form that serves you best

ABUNDANCE BEYOND MONEY

While money is often seen as the primary symbol of abundance, true abundance encompasses all areas of life:

- Health and vitality
- Loving relationships
- Creative inspiration
- Opportunities and synchronicities
- Time and freedom
- Knowledge and wisdom
- Joy and fulfillment

When you expand your definition of abundance to include all these forms, you begin to see that you are already abundant in many ways. This recognition shifts your vibration and attracts even more abundance into your life.

THE FIVE FORMS **of Abundance - Bashar:**

Bashar indicates that there are five forms of Abundance, and that source will often use a combination of these to reflect back to you your abundant state.

1. Financial Abundance - Money and currency flowing to you through expected and unexpected channels.

2. Trade and Barter - Receiving what you need through direct exchange of services, skills, or goods without monetary transaction.

3. Synchronicities - Perfect timing and "coincidences" that place exactly what you need in your path at the right moment.

4. Inspiration - Divine downloads and creative ideas that become valuable solutions, opportunities, or offerings.

5. Imagination - Visionary capacity that reveals new possibilities and pathways to receive what you desire.

THE FOUR PILLARS **of Abundance Consciousness**

Recognition: Seeing all forms of abundance as valid expressions of divine provision

Perception: Shifting focus from "I don't have" to "Abundance is already here"

Allowance: Letting go of the demand that abundance must come in a specific way

Appreciation: Gratitude aligns your energy to abundance, increasing its flow

MANIFESTING **Abundance in Practical Terms**

To manifest abundance, you must first become the abundance you seek. This is not pretending—it's remembering your divine nature as abundance itself.

1. Embody the Consciousness of Having, Not Seeking

Live from the fulfilled state, not the searching state. When you make decisions, ask: "What would I choose if I knew abundance was already mine?" What actions can you take now, with what you have. You may not be able to call the manufacturer to print the shirts that you want, but you can design them. This shifts you from chasing to receiving, from begging to accepting what has always been yours.

2. Surrender the How, Trust the Flow

Release your grip on the mechanism of delivery. Divine intelligence orchestrates through infinite channels—most of which your human mind cannot foresee. The divine can deliver your abundance in any of the five forms listed by Bashar. Don't close yourself off to say it only has to be money. Synchronicity could deliver you a person who has exactly what you need, without any money. Be open to however the Divine works! Your job is to hold the feeling; God's job is to handle the form.

3. Let Excitement Be Your Compass

Your genuine excitement is divine guidance in motion. It's your Higher Mind saying this is the way. Even on small items. It doesn't have to be your LIFE mission. It could be on what's for lunch today? Whichever holds the highest excitement, begin to follow the thread. It's not random—it's your soul's GPS toward your highest good. When you follow what lights you up, you automatically align with abundance because joy and abundance share the same frequency.

4. Appreciation as Creative Power

Appreciation isn't just thankfulness—it's active creation. When you appreciate what is, you literally increase its value in your experience. Gratitude is the multiplier of manifestation: what you genuinely appreciate, appreciates. This is literally financial interest accumulating on your behalf. Imagine each day appreciating because you have actively decided to appreciate as a physical grounding action towards everything and anything you can think of seen and unseen!

The Key Shift: Stop trying to get abundant and start remembering you are abundance expressing itself in human form. You are the Divine, it can be no other way. Well, it can, if you decide to line up with the lies about you.

COMMON BLOCKS **to Abundance**

UNWORTHINESS

The belief that you don't deserve abundance is one of the strongest blocks. Remember: your existence itself proves your worthiness.

Fear of Success

Sometimes people fear that having abundance will change them or their relationships in negative ways.

Guilt About Having More

The belief that having abundance means taking from others is based on scarcity thinking. Abundance is infinite.

Insistence on Specific Forms

Demanding that abundance come only as money, or only in certain ways, limits the universe's ability to provide.

Biblical Perspective on Abundance

The Bible contains numerous passages that support the understanding of divine abundance:

Matthew 6:26 (KJV): "Behold the fowls of the air: for they sow not, neither do they reap, nor gather into barns; yet your heavenly Father feedeth them. Are ye not much better than they?"

This verse reminds us that divine provision is natural and constant. If God provides for the birds, how much more will He provide for His children?

John 10:10 (KJV): "I am come that they might have life, and that they might have it more abundantly."

Jesus came to show us the path to abundant life—not just survival, but thriving in all areas.

Matthew 6:33 (KJV):

"But seek ye first the kingdom of God, and his righteousness; and all these things shall be added unto you."

When you prioritize spiritual alignment ("the kingdom of God" within you-Divine Knowing) and right living ("his righteousness or speaking what God says about you at all times,") your external needs naturally fall into place.

THE POWER **of Appreciation**

I'll close this chapter with a promise from Abraham Hicks that speaks to the transformative power of aligning with abundance through appreciation:

"It is our promise to you: if you write things you appreciate in others, in life, and in yourself, you will have such a dramatic change in 30 days; and if you continued for 6 months, the change will be so powerful, so strong, that others who know you will not recognize the old you." —Abraham

Your worthiness is inherent. Abundance is your natural state. The mirror is always reflecting. What are you choosing to embody?

CHAPTER 10 KEY TAKEAWAYS:

• Abundance is your natural state—it's about allowing, not acquiring

• Reality mirrors your internal relationship with worthiness and trust

• True abundance encompasses all areas of life, not just money

• Gratitude and appreciation are the fastest ways to shift into abundance consciousness

• Following your excitement aligns you with the natural flow of abundance

ELEVEN
CHAPTER 11: HEALTH

Health is not merely the absence of disease; it is the full alignment of body, mind, and spirit with the infinite intelligence of creation. Physical pain, illness, and imbalance often serve as signals—messages from the higher self—revealing areas of resistance, misalignment, or unprocessed emotions. By shifting one's perspective, embracing the body's natural intelligence, and allowing divine energy to flow, true healing can be realized.

The essence of self-love is recognizing that everything in our external reality is a reflection of our internal state. Bashar emphasizes that if one is not in love with oneself, it is impossible to fully love anything else. Every external experience mirrors aspects of ourselves that we need to understand. Rejecting parts of our external world means rejecting parts of ourselves that are calling for recognition and integration.

"If you're in love with yourself, and I don't mean in a narcissistic way, you will accept that whatever is going on in the way that it's unfolding has some information for you." —Bashar

The teachings stress that our beliefs and self-perceptions shape our experiences. If one believes they are unworthy, unloveable, or broken, these perceptions imprint on the body, influencing cellular function. The key to healing and transformation lies in self-acceptance, acknowledging the inherent perfection within, and allowing change to occur without resistance.

PHYSICAL PAIN **and Resistance to the Natural Self**

Pain is an indicator of resistance. Bashar explains that chronic pain results from resisting one's natural state of being. The physical body is designed to be in a state of ease, flow, and vitality. When one resists their natural expression—whether through fear, judgment, or conformity to external expectations—the body responds with discomfort, tension, and eventually illness.

Similarly, Dolores Cannon teaches that speaking to the body—acknowledging and expressing love toward one's cells—has a profound impact on well-being.

"The body loves for you to talk with it. You have an entire universe within you—all the cells and organs are going about their own thing, but if you begin to talk to it, tell everybody how much you love it—'I love you, heart. I love you, liver.' It loves that because somebody's paying attention to it." —Dolores Cannon

Since the human body is composed mostly of water, our self-talk directly influences the molecular structure of our very being. Negative self-perceptions, harsh inner dialogue, and fear-based thoughts alter the vibrational integrity of the body's water, contributing to illness. Conversely, self-love, gratitude, and positive affirmations restructure the body's water in a way that promotes healing and vitality.

"THE HIDDEN MESSAGES IN WATER" **by Masaru Emoto**

Dr. Masaru Emoto's work with water crystals presents one of the most visually striking illustrations of a principle we've explored throughout this book: consciousness affects reality.

Through his experiments photographing frozen water crystals, Emoto demonstrated that water exposed to positive words like "love," "gratitude," and "thank you" formed beautiful, symmetrical, and intricate crystal structures. Water exposed to negative words like "hate," "evil," and "you fool" formed chaotic, fragmented, and distorted crystals. Similarly, water exposed to classical music produced elegant formations, while heavy metal music resulted in disharmonious patterns. Even prayer and positive intention directed toward water appeared to create beautiful crystalline structures.

THE SCIENTIFIC CONTEXT

It's important to acknowledge that Emoto's experiments have not been validated through traditional peer-reviewed scientific methods. Critics from the scientific community point to the absence of controlled experimental conditions, potential experimenter bias, and lack of reproducible methodology. These are legitimate concerns that deserve recognition.

However, I offer Emoto's work here not as scientifically proven fact, but as a powerful contemplative framework that aligns remarkably with the principles we've explored throughout this book—the mirror principle, the law of reflection, vibrational frequency, and the relationship between consciousness and physical reality.

THE BODY AS WATER: **A Profound Consideration**

Here's what makes Emoto's work particularly relevant to our discussion: the human body is approximately 70% water.

Whether or not water crystals literally restructure themselves in response to consciousness, this question demands our attention: If we treated our thoughts and words as though they were directly affecting the 70% of our bodies that is water, how differently would we think and speak?

Consider the implications:

• Every thought you think is occurring in a body made mostly of water

• Every word you speak to yourself passes through a system that is 70% water

• Every emotion you feel reverberates through this liquid medium

If Emoto's principle holds even a fraction of truth—that consciousness affects water—then the quality of your inner dialogue is not merely psychological. It may be physiological.

ALIGNMENT with Established Principles

Emoto's framework aligns perfectly with what we already know:

The Mirror Principle: Just as reality mirrors your consciousness externally, your body may be mirroring it internally through the water that composes you.

Neville's Teaching: "Assume the feeling of the wish fulfilled" takes on new meaning when you consider that your body's water may be responding to and encoding that assumption.

The Law of Vibration: If everything is frequency and resonance, and water comprises most of your physical form, then your dominant frequency is quite literally shaping your physical structure moment by moment.

Biblical Wisdom: When Jesus spoke of "living water" (John 4:10-14) and when scripture speaks of being "washed by the word" (Ephesians 5:26), perhaps there is deeper wisdom than we initially understood.

The Practical Application: Live As If

Whether Emoto's experiments can be replicated in a double-blind scientific setting or not, the practical wisdom remains profoundly valuable:

What if you lived AS IF your words were restructuring your body's water?

Would you:

• Speak more kindly to yourself?

- Choose thoughts of gratitude over thoughts of complaint?
- Bless your body rather than criticize it?
- Drink water with intention and appreciation?
- Recognize that self-hatred is literally toxic to your physical form?

THE BLESSING of Water

Many spiritual traditions have long held water as sacred and have blessed it before consumption. Perhaps they understood something our modern world is only beginning to remember.

You can engage with this practice today:
- Before drinking water, hold the glass and express gratitude
- Speak words of health, vitality, and wellness over your water
- Recognize that you're not just hydrating—you're programming the primary substance of your physical form

As Emoto himself discovered, the most powerful words for creating beautiful water crystals were "love" and "gratitude." Not coincidentally, these are the same states that Scripture, spiritual teachers, and now quantum physics point to as the highest frequencies of consciousness.

A FRAMEWORK for Transformation

I present Emoto's work not as scientific dogma, but as an invitation: What if you treated your body—70% water—as a living crystal that responds to your consciousness?

This isn't about proving skeptics wrong or defending controversial experiments. This is about recognizing a pattern that appears again and again:
- Your words matter.
- Your thoughts shape reality.
- Your internal state affects your physical form.
- Gratitude and love create coherence.

• Negativity and hatred create chaos.

Whether the mechanism is water crystals, neural pathways, hormonal cascades, or vibrational frequency, the practical outcome remains the same: your consciousness affects your physical experience.

THE INVITATION

So I invite you to experiment for yourself:

For the next 30 days, speak to your body as though it is listening—because it is. Speak to your water as though it responds—because perhaps it does. Choose words of life, health, appreciation, and love.

Notice what changes.

Not because science has validated it, but because your own experience validates it. Not because critics approve, but because you are the authority in your own reality.

The mirror is always reflecting. Your body is always listening. The water within you is always responding.

What will you speak into it today?

FORGIVENESS, **Letting Go, and Cellular Alignment**

Forgiveness is a liberating force that frees the body from stored emotional trauma. Bashar explains that natural anger only lasts about 15 seconds—any emotion that lingers beyond that is judgment and invalidation.

"If anger lasts longer than 15 seconds, it's no longer natural—it's judgment of a negative type because you're invalidating something." —Bashar

Holding onto regret, grief, or resentment lowers the body's vibration, interfering with its ability to function optimally. Bashar suggests a unique technique: listening to the first three minutes of Beethoven's Symphony No. 7, Movement 2 while in a peaceful state. This composition is vibrationally aligned with letting go, forgiving oneself, and restoring harmony within.

BREATHWORK and Cellular Regeneration

Abraham's teachings highlight the power of breath in restoring well-being. Conscious breathing allows trillions of cells in the body to align with their natural rhythm, facilitating healing and balance.

"Breathe in. Breathe out. Your intelligent body is comprised of trillions of cells, seeking and finding alignment and balance at all times." —Abraham Hicks

Deep breathing releases resistance, fear, and tension, bringing the body into its natural state of well-being. When practiced consistently, breathwork can reverse chronic conditions, improve mental clarity, and strengthen the body's energetic connection to Source.

THE POWER of Knowing and How Self-Talk Affects the Body

Your knowingness—the internal dialogue you hold about yourself —has a direct impact on the cellular structure of your body. Every thought sends energetic signals to the cells, influencing their function and regenerative capabilities.

Bashar and other teachings emphasize that the body does not exist inside the mind—the body is the mind in physical form. You are not a physical being that has a soul; you are a soul expressing itself in physical form.

"Your physical body is your spirit in physical terminology. So being physical doesn't mean you're not spiritual." —Bashar

By shifting self-talk toward empowerment, love, and gratitude, one rewires the body's cellular programming. Disease is often a result of misaligned thought patterns, and the cure lies in aligning with divine knowing—the certainty that health, joy, and abundance are your birthright.

. . .

LIVING **in Alignment**

Living a life of health, abundance, and harmony requires a shift from fear-based existence to divine knowing. This transformation happens when one:

- Accepts their present reality without resistance
- Loves and communicates with their body as an extension of their consciousness
- Detoxifies both physically and mentally, removing toxins and limiting beliefs
- Engages in breathwork to return to a natural state of cellular alignment
- Uses self-talk intentionally, ensuring thoughts are nourishing and empowering
- Lets go of emotional burdens through forgiveness, music, and meditation
- Understands that the body's water reflects the mind, and cultivates loving thoughts

When these principles are integrated, one moves from a state of healing to a state of thriving, living as a fully realized divine being in harmony with creation.

"The kingdom of God is within you." —Luke 17:21 (KJV)

PRACTICAL APPLICATION: **Daily Spiritual Health Practice**

Bashar's formula is really the formula. This portion of the formula that I'm talking about is how I come back to myself daily. Before going to bed I center myself, I appreciate all the good things that I can think about and I relax and trust that all things are working in my favor. In the morning first thing, again I wake up and look for things to appreciate to elevate my vibration, I meditate sometimes, and center myself with positive appreciating thoughts on my morning walk and I come back to myself, remembering who and what I am. It's a spiritual practice, my daily ritual.

THE KING/QUEEN **and the Fool: Choosing Your Inner Voice**

Rising in vibration is simple to grasp. A quick analogy is this: Each woman or man has two people in them—the King/Queen and the fool. Whoever you speak to is who is going to respond to you. I speak to the King in myself. I speak to the God in me. I speak words of light, love, and empowerment into myself. I speak the work of God over me and through me. Speaking the word of light and love over myself is raising my vibrations. Speaking from an authentic place of happiness and appreciation is getting on the high flying disk.

ANOTHER EXAMPLE: Throughout the day you will have the opportunity to tune your tuner to many different television channels or frequencies. This is your choice. This is your freedom. This is your power. I choose frequencies or Television channels that offer laughter/comedies. That offer upliftment. I choose my thoughts wisely. Not all the times, but I choose and re-choose and re-choose daily. Once you get practiced in choosing these higher frequencies you become acclimated to them and they become your new set point. Then you flow from there. That is a lightness of being when you can authentically be you with little effort. It's wonderful.

NOTE ON HEALTH:

Often, people live in a hellish way for decades and then wish to heal themselves in two months by doing what is so-called "right." This information I'm providing is not a "magic cure" to your ills—this is a way of life, a lifestyle. If you are dealing with physical ailments, it is wise to consult your doctor, especially if you have programmed yourself to do so. I am not suggesting that this information will heal you versus going to the doctor or seeking professional medical assistance. I am suggesting that forming healthy spiritual, mental, emotional, psychological, and financial habits early in life will go a long way toward preventing serious ailments in all these areas to begin with. As the saying goes, "An ounce of prevention is worth a pound of cure."

We have not been taught healthy ways to think or healthy ways to be. Often, many of us are in survival mode, just trying to make it through the day, the week, the month.

There is no magical cure for anything in your life. All of it requires you to do the work. Yes, there are Miracles! Absolutely! Any and every Miracle, that I've ever experienced, I wasn't betting on it to happen. However, why would you put yourself in a situation where only a miracle would be needed in order for you to keep going?

This is not spiritual "woo woo." This is not make-believe. This is your life. And what you put into it, you will get out of it.

CHAPTER 11 KEY TAKEAWAYS:

• Health is the alignment of body, mind, and spirit with divine intelligence

• Self-love and positive self-talk directly influence cellular function and healing

• Forgiveness releases stored emotional trauma and restores vibrational harmony

• Breathwork aligns trillions of cells with their natural healing rhythm

• Daily spiritual practice maintains high-frequency alignment and well-being

• You have the power to choose which inner voice to nurture - the King/Queen or the fool

• Consistent practice of choosing higher frequencies creates a new, elevated set point

TWELVE

CHAPTER 12: FEAR AND ANXIETY: A MESSENGER FOR REALIGNMENT AND GROWTH

Your Energy is Not Neutral—It is Naturally High-Vibrational

Your natural state is one of excitement, joy, love, clarity, focus and high-frequency energy. This is the essence of your being. However, reality itself is neutral—it is simply a mirror reflecting your internal state. You have the opportunity to exist on either side of the neutrality based on the mix of emotions when derived from your beliefs on a multitude of subjects.

Fear and anxiety do not exist as enemies or obstacles; they serve as valuable messengers, signaling a misalignment between your current perception and your true self. You can adopt this understanding as you begin to understand that life is happening for you, not to you.

When fear or anxiety arises, it does not always mean something is "wrong"—it could simply indicate that a belief you hold is filtering your energy in a way that is out of harmony with your natural, high-vibrational state. Instead of resisting these emotions, you can embrace them as guides, showing you where you need to shift your definitions and perspectives. It is important to understand that I am not speaking about imminent fear. I am not talking about the fear that comes from someone robbing or attempting to harm you. I am speaking of catching fear or anxiety early, when it's just a thought or a worry. The important thing to realize is that if FEAR is not properly acknowledged or addressed, it may go away, but it will come back bigger and stronger until it gets your attention. You must acknowledge the fear and "transmute" it in order to properly address fear. What do I mean by transmute fear?

Say you make the mistake of watching the news one day and you hear about a war that is going on in some part of the world. How do I utilize this concept to handle this fear that may arise? 1st it's important to note that, it would be better if you had not introduced these subjects into your reality, as energy flows where attention goes. I once read a quote that said. "Energy is the currency of the universe, when you pay attention to anything you buy that experience" – Author Unknown. This is true. And even more important to understand, this IS how the universe works. When you watch the news and hear about the 1 murder that happened in a city of 13 million, you are adding that experience or buying that experience for yourself, and mixing it with your vibration. Do this enough times, and you will find that negative experience will begin to get closer and closer to you until it IS something that is present in your daily thoughts. Now when you go to the store up the street, you are "on guard" and "on the lookout," all because you've spent years watching over sensationalized news about bad events that have happened far far away from you, and you now have mixed these experiences into the truth of your reality. As Abraham has indicated, Enlightenment is not a college degree, meaning "once you attain it, you will always have it." It is something you must choose daily.

You must daily cultivate the garden of you mind, only focusing and adding in high vibrational content when possible. Understand you are responsible for your mix of emotion, and your mix of emotion determines your "aura," your vibrational resonance. You can change these vibrational habits, however it's important to understand that just as these habits were not built over night, they do not magically go away overnight. It takes commitment and accountability to what you are spiritually feeding yourself.

As Abraham has also often said, when you haven't dealt with the negative momentum that you have created and that momentum has caught up with you.... It's just like jumping out of an airplane without a parachute. Hang on, It will be over soon. Or not, but you get the point.

People that don't manage their emotions or their momentum, don't like to own their results, but it's important that you hear the truth about your power, and understand how to use it to better your life. Remember this is a master class, you are here to learn how to consciously manifest. You are here to transmute your darkness into light, and through the process learn the lessons that are being taught. You are here to discover the divine from a new perspective, having forgotten your true identity.

FEAR AS AN ALARM BELL—LET **It Work for You**

When you catch fear early, you can think of fear and anxiety as an internal alarm system. They are not punishments, nor do they indicate failure. Instead, they are signals prompting you to examine an internal belief that is out of alignment with your core essence.

• When anxiety appears, pause and ask: "What belief must I be holding for this fear to exist?"

• If you allow yourself to listen, your reality will reflect back the answer

• Once you identify the belief, you can choose to shift it into one that aligns with your natural state of joy, love, and excitement

Fear is not a block; it is a doorway. When you acknowledge it as an ally and a friend, rather than an adversary, it transforms into curiosity, exploration, and ultimately, clarity. Why is this understanding so important?

. . .

THE FOURTH LAW **and the Mirror Reality**

The Fourth Law states: "What you put out is what you get back." This means that your external experiences are not random—they are precise reflections of your internal state. If you radiate fear, insecurity, or lack, you will encounter experiences that reinforce those states. If you align with excitement, trust, and love, your reality will reflect those energies back to you.

Now the question is "I've ignored fear for years, and now it is big and scary, how do I handle it? Well there are a couple of techniques that can be utilized. First it would be wise to attempt any action related to fear from a state of confidence and alignment. Meaning from a high flying place. You want to be in a good mental and emotional state to begin with. You want to be connected to your power source and plugged in. Once you are, you can then address the validity of the fear. Invite fear in and examine the situation. Examine, if the fear has been born of worry, and anxiety, or if it's actually something that is real and true for you now. If it has been born of worry and anxiety, Bashar states that the moment the negative thought appears to be unaligned, and "nonsensical" meaning its meaning is not rational, it disappears. Meaning the moment that you look at the basics of why you had the fear and it doesn't logically even make sense, it loses its power and dissipates.

A good exercise or question that I got from Bashar, is to ask yourself when examining your beliefs around this specific subject is. "What would I have to believe is true about this situation in order for me to have this fear or this _____?" Once you sit in silence with this question concerning the subject you will give way to the answer, if you are honest and are wanting the solution. The answer will point either to a nonsensical understanding that is not valid, or it will point to a deeper belief that needs to be addressed. Bashar indicates that this exercise typically points to a lack of worthiness and self love at the root or core of the problem.

The truth of reality is that you are the only person in your world, and everyone, and everything else in your world is made of your own energy for the purpose of your growth. If you understand this you can begin to use your power to label circumstances and situations properly. This is important as you determine "What you put out," and thus what you get back. If you encounter a situation that is negative, and you put out. "Well, I'm not really sure why this is happening," but since I know that "all things work together for good to them that love God" (Romans 8:28), I will maintain that this situation is going to serve me in a positive way, that situation must then serve you in a positive way. Not right away, necessarily. But, if you maintain a true conviction that this situation, which is made up of your own energy, was created to serve you in a positive way, as you are "god," it must serve you in a positive way.

Here's a personal example from my life of how I learned to "eat the meat and throw away the bones" when dealing with difficult teachers and situations. In life you will encounter all types of people. Being spiritual doesn't exempt you for life. It instead should enable you to navigate it more successfully.

Eating the meat and throwing the bones away is a valuable lesson that you must learn in order to function as a human in the world. Humans are often flawed as we are learning and all in process. A prime example is my Father. He was a bipolar, manic-depressive, alcoholic Vietnam veteran with PTSD. Needless to say as a father, and husband he was not good. To put it politely. Even if these efforts were his best foot forward, they failed abysmally, in comparison to what I wanted or wished for.

Now as a teacher, he was a master class of information alone. He first hand taught me so many things NOT to do, by watching his example. He is the reason I have stuck it out in my marriage, and have not done so many negative things from excessive drinking to being physically abusive to others. etc. I learned to "eat the meat" meaning learn from the subject at hand, without taking personal where the message was coming from.

Now that you've come to understand, How empowering these spiritual teachings are you, can easily see how they correspond to what Jesus was really intending to say as you can now understand it from a higher perspective.

THE 4 C'S: **Your Framework for Transforming Challenges BASHAR**

WHEN OBSTACLES ARISE on your path, remember: nothing appears by accident. Every circumstance unfolding before you is precisely what must occur at this moment. You arranged this very situation along your journey—so why would you respond with negativity when you understand something beneficial awaits you within it?

This is where the 4 C's become your transformative framework:

CALMNESS

Maintain your center. Breathe. Ground yourself in the recognition that this moment serves you.

CONFIDENCE

Trust with unwavering certainty that valuable wisdom exists within this experience. Something meaningful is present for you to discover and integrate.

CURIOSITY (LIKE A CHILD)

Approach this with wonder and openness:
• What wisdom might this contain?

• I'm genuinely intrigued—what could this teach me about my expansion?

• How might this propel me toward greater understanding?

• There's something remarkable about this challenge presenting itself right now.

CREATIVITY

Engage your imagination and innovative thinking when encountering obstacles:

• What unique approach resonates with my authentic self?

• How can I extract value from this by engaging it in ways others might not consider?

• Remain willing to be adaptable, receptive, and wonder-filled

• Extract from each challenge exactly what will elevate you

THE KEY **to Maintaining Positive State:**

"I may not yet understand why this is manifesting, but I know with certainty it will benefit me in meaningful ways."

Since you recognize there are no random occurrences—that what's unfolding is exactly what needs to unfold—this means you yourself designed this challenge as part of your evolutionary pathway. Given this understanding, why would you respond with resistance or negativity when you know something constructive is embedded within it for your discovery?

By comprehending this mechanism—by truly knowing how reality operates—you naturally maintain an elevated state. This understanding itself becomes the foundation for staying aligned, empowered, and open to the gifts each challenge brings.

GOD'S WILL **IS Your Will: Understanding Divine Free Will**

There's a fundamental misunderstanding that needs to be addressed: **God's will is your will—because there is no difference between you and Source.** You are an expression of Source itself. This means the entire concept of free will is simply this: **you get to determine how you experience reality.**

And here's what makes this so profound: **the universe is unconditionally supportive. Unconditionally.**

When you understand what that word truly means, you realize that when you choose to accept a limiting belief, creation responds with, "Alright, I'll support you in that"—and it magnifies and amplifies what you've decided is true. If you approach something with negativity, the universe mirrors that back to you.

But equally, when you choose to approach circumstances with a positive perspective, the universe responds identically: "Okay, I will unconditionally support you in what you've declared as true."

This is why it's so essential to become aware of what you actually believe and why you're holding onto specific beliefs. **The universe has no agenda except to reflect back to you what you've claimed is true**—because it is unconditionally supportive of your choices.

The universe functions as a mirror, completely and totally. If you look into a physical mirror and see yourself frowning, that reflection reveals you're wearing a frown. The mirror cannot display a smile until you smile first. Reality operates identically. When you observe circumstances that aren't serving you, look within and recognize that's what you're projecting—whether you're conscious of it or not.

This is why investigating your own consciousness becomes so crucial. Connect with what you're genuinely emanating, what you're truly broadcasting, because we can deceive ourselves. We might convince ourselves that our anxiety is actually excitement when it isn't, while we're actually surrendering to fear-based beliefs. And the universe reflects that back as feedback, as a guideline so you can understand: "This is what you're doing."

If you want to witness the reflection change—if you

want the frown in the mirror to shift—you must smile first. The mirror cannot transform before you do.

THIS MIRROR PRINCIPLE **reveals something even more profound about your relationship with the Divine:**

THE TRUTH IS FAR MORE EMPOWERING: When you align with your authentic nature, your will becomes the expression of divine will. You are not separate from God—you ARE God experiencing itself through your unique perspective. Therefore, your genuine desires, your excitement, your joy—these are not distractions from God's plan; they are the mechanism through which divine will expresses itself in your life.

This is why Jesus declared, "I and my Father are one" (John 10:30). He wasn't claiming exclusive divinity—he was demonstrating what happens when a soul fully remembers its unity with Source. When you operate from this recognition, the question "Is this my will or God's will?" dissolves completely. There is no conflict. Your authentic excitement IS divine guidance. Your true desires ARE the universe calling you toward your highest expression.

The illusion of separation creates the belief that you must sacrifice your wants to serve God's wants. But Divine Knowing reveals the truth: God's will for you is that you remember who you are and live from that knowing. Your joy, your fulfillment, your expansion—this IS what the Divine desires for you, because you ARE the Divine experiencing itself. When you follow your highest excitement with integrity, you are literally following divine will in its purest form.

This doesn't mean every fleeting impulse or fear-based desire represents divine will. It means that when you align with your Higher Mind—when you follow genuine excitement rather than addiction or escape—you are tuning into the same intelligence that orchestrates galaxies, the same creative force that breathes life into all existence. And that force is not separate from you. It IS you, expressing through you, creating as you.

So stop waiting for permission. Stop asking if it's "God's will" as if God were somewhere out there judging your choices. **You are the expression of divine will.** Your authentic path, your true calling, your genuine joy—this is God experiencing itself as you. And when you step fully into that truth, the universe moves with you, not against you.

CHAPTER 12 KEY TAKEAWAYS:

- **Fear and anxiety are messengers signaling misalignment, not enemies to fight**—they show you where beliefs need examination and transformation
- **Your natural state is high-vibrational joy, love, and excitement**—any deviation from this reveals beliefs filtering your authentic frequency
- **The 4 C's provide your framework for transforming challenges**: Calmness (maintain center), Confidence (trust wisdom exists within this), Curiosity (childlike wonder about the lesson), Creativity (unique approaches that serve your growth)
- **Challenges are not accidents—you designed them as part of your evolutionary pathway**—why respond with negativity when something beneficial awaits discovery?
- **God's will IS your will because there is no difference between you and Source**—you are an expression of Source itself, and free will means you define your experience
- **The universe is unconditionally supportive of whatever you choose**—it magnifies and amplifies whatever beliefs you accept as true, whether limiting or empowering
- **Reality functions as a complete mirror**—it cannot show you a smile until you smile first; external change requires internal transformation first
- **The Fourth Law ensures your external reality**

mirrors your internal state—what you observe "out there" reflects what you're projecting from within

• **Following authentic excitement (not fear-based impulses) IS following divine will**—when aligned with your Higher Mind, your desires are the universe calling you toward highest expression

THIRTEEN

CHAPTER 13: JESUS: THE TRUTH BEYOND THE MISINTERPRETATIONS

The Journey to Understanding

In my many years of studying Jesus, the Bible, and the world's diverse spiritual traditions—from the canonical Gospels to the Gnostic texts of Nag Hammadi, from the Dead Sea Scrolls and the teachings of the Essenes to the Hermetic wisdom of Egypt, from the Vedas of India to the path of the Buddha, from the ecstatic love of the Sufi mystics to the contemplative traditions of Christian mystics—I've come to understand Jesus in a way that honors both history and deeper truth.

The historical texts—both canonical and non-canonical—present Jesus as the Christ, the Messiah, the anointed one who fulfilled divine promise. This is documented. This is foundational. I do not dispute this.

But I have also come to see that Jesus represents something more —the archetype of complete divine-human integration. He attained full oneness with Source and lived that reality so completely that he became the demonstration of what is possible when a soul fully remembers and embodies its divine nature.

This understanding doesn't replace traditional faith—it expands it. It invites us to see Jesus not as an exception separated from humanity by an unbridgeable gap, but as the firstborn among many—the one who walked the path first and showed us it could be walked.

The mystical and esoteric traditions—from the Gnostic writings to the contemplative streams within Christianity itself—consistently point to this dual reality: Jesus as both divine Savior and spiritual exemplar. These texts emphasize inner transformation, direct knowing, and the potential for union with the Divine. They present Jesus not as someone to worship from a distance, but as a guide showing the way home.

In this light, Jesus stands as both the Christ and the Teacher—a being who, through perfect alignment with divine truth, revealed the path of awakening available to every soul willing to walk it through love, surrender, and conscious remembrance.

This is what I have come to know. Not to diminish who he was, but to honor the fullness of what he came to show us.

This perspective has been shaped not only through study, but through lived experience—through moments of silence, surrender, and insight where truth revealed itself beyond words. In these moments, I began to see the golden thread running through all traditions: In the Gospel of Thomas, Jesus speaks of the light already within us. In the Bhagavad Gita, Krishna reveals the Self as the eternal witness. In the Tao Te Ching, the Source flows through all things as their very nature. In Hildegard of Bingen's visions, the Divine pulses as living greenness in every soul. In Rumi's ecstatic verse, the Beloved is discovered as the very breath within the seeker.

Different languages. Different cultures. Different times.

But one truth: the Divine is not distant—it is here, intimate, alive, and inseparable from who you are.

What I share is not doctrine. It is an invitation—to see Christ not as an exception, but as a reflection. Not a figure to exalt above ourselves, but a reminder of what it means to come home to who and what we truly are.

. . .

THE MISUNDERSTOOD SAVIOR

One of the most profound misunderstandings in religious tradition centers on a single question: Is Jesus a Savior?

The answer is unequivocally yes—but not in the way institutional religion has portrayed it.

When Jesus declared, "The works that I do shall he do also; and greater works than these shall he do" (John 14:12), he wasn't speaking in metaphor. He was stating a fact about human potential.

When he identified himself as "the firstborn among many brethren" (Romans 8:29), he was pointing to our shared divine nature —he was first, not alone.

When he proclaimed, "I and my Father are one" (John 10:30), he was demonstrating alignment with Source, not claiming exclusive divinity that no one else could access.

And when he taught, "Seek ye first the kingdom of God, and his righteousness; and all these things shall be added unto you" (Matthew 6:33), he was revealing a path—a direct route to divine knowing available to all who would walk it.

Yet somehow, these crystal-clear teachings have been twisted into a narrative that separates Jesus from humanity rather than connecting us to the same power he embodied.

Scripture itself warns against this distortion: "Having a form of godliness, but denying the power thereof" (2 Timothy 3:5). This is precisely what happens when we worship Jesus from a distance while rejecting the truth that we hold the same divine potential within ourselves.

This is saviorhood through remembrance, not rescue.

Jesus came to mirror the divine potential within us all—to demonstrate that we are not broken sinners awaiting salvation, but expressions of the Infinite who have temporarily forgotten our true nature.

He was the prototype, not the exception. The first, not the only.

His life demonstrated what happens when a soul fully activates its divine nature—when one stops seeking God "out there" and recognizes the truth within: I and my Father are one.

This is not blasphemy. This is the truth that sets you free.

When you align with this understanding—when you stop denying the power thereof and start embodying it—you step into the same creative authority Jesus demonstrated.

Not through intellectual belief alone, but through embodied alignment—through the resonance that occurs when your thoughts, feelings, and actions harmonize with Divine Love, Clarity, and Truth.

JESUS AS EXAMPLE, **Not Exception**

So let's get down to it. Is Jesus a Savior? Yes, he is a Savior. But not in the way people try to make it seem.

He's not Superman coming back to save us. No. He provided the example of the way in which you have to be in order to know the light that he talked about. That's why he said, "These things and greater shall you do."

Think about it: You can't do "these things and greater" if you don't have the connection, the power that he has. So either he was lying when he said that, or people have fundamentally misunderstood what he meant.

Jesus is a Savior because he's an example of who we're supposed to be—an example of how we're supposed to be. He's "the firstborn among many brethren"—the first to fully awaken and demonstrate what's possible, pointing the way for all who would follow.

The important thing we get from this understanding is how to be, not what to worship, but how to align.

Much of what we have been taught about Jesus has been shaped by institutions that wanted to control the narrative. When he said, "I am the way, the truth, and the life" (John 14:6), he was not elevating himself above humanity—he was revealing what is possible within humanity. He was saying that we could and should align the way he aligned, if our intent is to be empowered. Do it this way. Be this way. I am the way, "do what I do." I am the truth, "say what I say," claim your divinity, your oneness the way I claim my oneness or alignment. I am the light, be an example of alignment, the way you see me being an example. Align with what the Father says about you. I am the way the truth and the light, no man come unto the Father but by me. This means that the only way you can connect to the Divine is through your inner alignment, embodying the feeling and the emotional frequency of love, of clarity, of understanding. It's the only way to re-connect the circuit of remembrance to your true power.

He called himself the "firstborn among many brothers," pointing to the truth that we are all capable of aligning with God, stepping into our higher selves, and embodying divine truth. Since he is the firstborn, who is the second, the third? Are we only born again once we die? What sense does that make. To be born again is to awaken as a new man, through understanding of the truth of who you are. Being washed by the water is an esoteric analogy that speaks of spiritual understanding.

Through deliberate manipulation of his story, Jesus was turned into something other—something superhuman. They made him untouchable, like a spiritual Superman separated from ordinary humanity. And yet, that was never his purpose or intent.

Ask yourself this one important question: Which understanding of Jesus provides the clearest path to allowing all of humanity to reach its highest timeline? Which version empowers people to become, versus looking outside themselves for someone to "save" them, with a prescribed middle man?

The true purpose of Christ was to awaken us to our own divinity —to help us reconnect to the truth of who we are: beings capable of walking in love, power, wisdom, and unity with God. He wanted us to follow his example, to move into our higher self, to align with our highest timeline. To remember our oneness. To become "god".

TRUE POWER **and Alignment**

True power flows from vibrational and emotional alignment—not from intellect alone, not from tradition, not from performance, not from position. It comes from a heart that feels God, a mind that chooses peace, a voice that speaks light, and hands that heal what they touch.

This is the true power thereof. And it is not reserved for the few, the chosen, or the righteous-by-name. It is available to any soul willing to remember the truth:

"The kingdom of God is within you." — Luke 17:21

So to every leader, every teacher, every preacher who claims the badge of Christ: What are your fruits?

Do your words heal or harm? Do your actions unite or divide? Do your deeds lift up or tear down? Does your presence bring peace or fear? Does your teaching empower or control?

Because Jesus made it clear: "By their fruits ye shall know them." — Matthew 7:20

And if your fruits are judgment, condemnation, division, fear, and control—then you are not producing the fruits of the Spirit, which are love, joy, peace, longsuffering, gentleness, goodness, faith, meekness, and temperance. — Galatians 5:22-23

So choose today: Will you keep clanging your cymbal—or will you become the tuning fork of the Divine? Will you continue having a form of godliness while denying the power? Or will you activate the divine knowing within you, align with Love, and step into the same authority Jesus demonstrated—not through position, but through presence?

The choice, as always, is yours.

QUESTION:

Now, you might be asking: if Jesus made this so clear, how did we end up so far from his actual teaching? That's the question we need to answer.

. . .

THE STRATEGIC SUPPRESSION **of Truth**

Let us use basic common sense for a moment. Imagine Jesus was alive today—in 2025, walking the streets of the United States. He has maybe twelve close followers. He is talking about, "My kingdom is coming soon."

At first? No big deal. The President would not feel threatened. The media would not care. People would say, "Oh, he is just another spiritual guy, just another voice in the crowd."

But then things start to change. Stories start to spread. This man is healing the sick, performing miracles. People claim he has raised the dead, opened blind eyes, grown back limbs, delivered people from mental torment.

Whether you interpret those miracles literally or metaphorically —whether he is raising people from physical death or awakening them from spiritual ignorance—that is beside the point.

The point is this: He is doing the unthinkable. He is drawing massive crowds. His words are cutting through the lies of the system. His message is not just spiritual—it is political. He is telling people, "The kingdom is within you." He is shaking the foundation of power, not with weapons, but with truth.

Now think like the Emperor. Think like the Roman elite back then—the same power structure that would eventually orchestrate Jesus's crucifixion. Would you just sit back and let that slide? Would you let a man who is proving the divine within himself and inspiring the masses to awaken the divine in themselves continue unchecked?

No. You eliminate him. And not just him. You erase the evidence, bury the scrolls, rebrand his teachings into doctrine that fits your structure of control. You do not leave behind a roadmap that empowers others to become like him. You rewrite the story. You mythologize him—you turn him into a God so high, so untouchable, no one dares try to follow in his footsteps.

Ask yourself: How does someone like the Emperor come to power in the first place? Through bribery, conquest, manipulation, and bloodshed. He ruled through fear and political maneuvering. So would a man like that preserve the truth of a divine teacher who could set people free from control? Or would he twist that truth, tame that truth, chain that truth—and call it "religion"?

I am just asking. You tell me.

UNDERSTANDING CHRIST CONSCIOUSNESS

When Jesus declared, "The works that I do shall he do also; and greater works than these shall he do" (John 14:12), this was not metaphor—it was direct teaching about human potential.

Jesus showed us that when we operate from divine knowing rather than limitation, what appear as miracles become natural expressions of aligned consciousness.

The True Second Coming

The "Second Coming of Christ" is not about an external return of a singular figure. It is the awakening of Christ Consciousness within every individual—the realization that:

• We are not separate from God
• We are divine beings in human form
• We hold the same power Jesus demonstrated

There is a second coming every time someone awakens to their true knowing of who they are—their Christ Consciousness.

This journey of humanity is moving from forgetfulness to remembrance. In the past, only a few individuals fully grasped these truths, but now, as collective consciousness expands, more souls are stepping into their divine awareness.

FROM FAITH **to Divine Knowing**

Traditional faith implies belief in something unseen. But Jesus operated from absolute knowing. He didn't pray for intervention; he commanded reality with certainty:

• "Be healed"
• "Peace, be still"

• "Lazarus, come forth"

This wasn't arrogance but alignment with divine law. Reality responds to conviction, not pleading.

The scriptures confirm this:

"It is your faith that has made you whole" (Luke 8:48)

"In his hometown, he could do no miracles because they did not believe" (Mark 6:4-6)

Those who saw only "the carpenter's son" couldn't receive miracles because their belief systems blocked reception. This demonstrates the Fourth Law—external reality mirrors internal conviction. To shift reality, one must first shift belief.

When you align with divine knowing rather than limitation—when you remove the blocks of doubt and step into certainty—miracles become the natural outcome of elevated consciousness.

THE KINGDOM WITHIN: **Present Reality, Not Future Promise**

"The Kingdom of God is within you" (Luke 17:21)

This isn't a future promise. It's present reality.

The Kingdom is a state of consciousness—the recognition of your divine nature. Salvation isn't something you await; it's something you embody.

Divine knowing transcends faith because it operates from the certainty that everything exists in the eternal now (Third Law). Jesus accessed this timeless perspective where healing and miracles are already present realities.

The Kingdom is not a place—it is a state of alignment with your true divine nature.

And it is here. Now. Within you.

BEYOND SEPARATION: **Remembering Oneness**

"Ye are gods; and all of you are children of the most High" (Psalm 82:6)

This aligns with the Second Law: The One is the All, and the All is the One.

A major misconception in religious doctrine is the belief in separation—between God and humanity, between good and evil, between heaven and earth. Jesus's true teachings dissolve these illusions.

What we call "Satan" isn't a separate being but an archetype of fear—the absence of divine love, representing the illusion of separation from Source. In truth, there is only one Source, one energy, one divine essence expressing itself through infinite forms.

Fear, suffering, and limitation arise when we forget this unity. Love, joy, and enlightenment emerge when we remember.

When you align with the Five Laws, fear dissolves—because you remember your eternal, unified, and powerful nature.

LIVING **the Christ Path**

So what does it mean to actually walk this path? To embody what Jesus demonstrated?

It means recognizing your divine nature – You exist eternally as an expression of infinite consciousness (First Law)

It means embracing oneness – You are not separate from the Divine or from each other (Second Law)

It means living in the now – The Kingdom, the power, the miracle—all exist in this present moment (Third Law)

It means creating through belief – Reality conforms to your conviction. Align your consciousness, and watch reality shift (Fourth Law)

It means constant transformation – This isn't a destination. It's an ongoing awakening, an ever-deepening alignment (Fifth Law)

To love unconditionally is to see beyond illusions, to recognize the divine essence in all beings, and to hold no judgment. When Jesus said, "Father, forgive them, for they know not what they do"

(Luke 23:34), he was demonstrating that love—true alignment—transcends resentment, fear, and separation.

Forgiveness isn't about excusing harm. It's about releasing attachment to suffering. It's about shifting your frequency so that reality can mirror back love instead of conflict.

THE EMPOWERING TRUTH

Jesus demonstrated that we are not separate from God. He showed that reality responds to consciousness, that miracles are natural expressions of alignment, and that the Kingdom exists within.

His life was a blueprint—not to be worshipped from afar, but to be followed, embodied, and expanded upon.

When he said we would do "greater works," he meant it.

The Christ consciousness he embodied is not exclusive. It is our birthright.

You don't need permission. You don't need an intermediary. You don't need to wait for a second coming outside yourself.

The second coming happens within you, the moment you remember who you are.

So the question isn't whether you're worthy of this power. The question is: Will you claim it?

Will you step into alignment?

Will you embody divine knowing?

Will you become the living demonstration of Christ Consciousness—not through religious performance, but through the resonance of love, clarity, and truth?

The choice has always been yours.

And the power has always been within you.

CHAPTER KEY TAKEAWAYS

• Jesus came to awaken humanity to its divine nature through example, not to be worshipped as separate and untouchable

• The institutional narrative was strategically shaped to control rather than empower

• Christ Consciousness is available to all—we hold the same creative power Jesus demonstrated

• The Kingdom of God is within—a present state of consciousness, not a future destination

• Direct connection to the Divine is your birthright—no intermediary required

• Reality responds to conviction and aligned belief—the Fourth Law in action

• The Five Laws provide the framework for embodying Christ consciousness

• Divine knowing transcends faith—it operates from certainty in the eternal now

• The second coming happens within each soul that awakens to its true nature

FOURTEEN

CHAPTER 14: THE FORMULA - YOUR LIBERATION MANUAL

Why This Chapter Exists

I've made a deliberate choice to dedicate an entire chapter to Bashar's Formula—and here's why:

If you grasp nothing else from this book but master this one teaching, your life will transform completely.

This is what I've experienced in my own life. The very book you're reading right now is a direct result of following this Formula— following my excitement to share what I've learned, taking it as far as I can, with no attachment to outcome, maintaining a positive state throughout, and trusting the synchronicities that brought it into being.

The Formula is the simplest, most direct path to alignment I have ever encountered. It cuts through all the complexity, all the philosophy, all the spiritual gymnastics—and gives you a clear, actionable roadmap for flowing with existence itself.

Joseph Campbell said it simply: "Follow your bliss."

Bashar says it with precision: Follow The Formula.

Both point to the same truth—but The Formula gives you the exact mechanism, the step-by-step instructions for how to do it.

This chapter could change everything for you.

THE FORMULA: **An Instruction Manual for Reality**

Bashar emphasizes that The Formula is not a philosophy to contemplate—it is a **precise instruction manual for navigating reality** in alignment with universal principles.

It is a mechanism. An exact method of co-creation with existence itself.

Each step operates like a key, unlocking the deeper workings of synchronicity, manifestation, and the interconnected structure of reality. This isn't wishful thinking. **This is the fundamental physics of how existence operates.**

THE FIVE CORE **Steps of The Formula**

These five steps form an interconnected system that activates the driving engine of your life. When practiced together, they create a positive chain reaction that restructures your reality to harmonize with your true self.

Step 1: Act on Your Highest Passion, Excitement, or Curiosity

In every moment, you have options. Among them, one always carries more excitement, more energy, more curiosity than the rest.

It doesn't have to be grand. It doesn't have to be ambitious. It might be:

- Calling a friend
- Riding your bike
- Taking a shower
- Taking a break
- Watching your favorite show
- Simply resting

. . .

EXCITEMENT IS **the language of your Higher Mind.** It's not random. It's not frivolous. It's your internal compass pointing toward your True North—the direction of your soul's highest alignment.

When you respond to this signal, you are declaring to the universe: *"I hear you. I trust you. I am ready."*

And the universe responds in kind.

STEP 2: **Act on It to the Best of Your Ability—Take It as Far as You Can**

No half measures. No holding back.

Invest your complete energy, dedication, and focus into it. Go all in. Take it as far as it will naturally go.

When the excitement fades, pause and ask yourself:

• Have I encountered a limiting belief that's diminishing my passion?

• Or has this path genuinely reached its natural conclusion?

If it's truly complete, transition to the next most exciting option.

Your passion is a breadcrumb trail. Each action leads to the next. Follow it with full commitment, and watch the path reveal itself one step at a time.

STEP 3: **Take This Action with Absolutely Zero Insistence on the Outcome**

Surrender control.

This is where most people stumble. They follow their excitement —but then grip tightly to how they think it should unfold.

Here's the truth: **The Physical Mind cannot foresee how events will develop.** It doesn't have the capacity. It can't see around corners. It doesn't know what synchronicities are being arranged on your behalf.

Only the Higher Mind—your soul's intelligence—grasps the larger perspective of your journey.

When you insist on a specific outcome, you block the flow. You cut off possibilities you can't even imagine. You tell the universe, *"No, do it MY way"*—and the universe steps back and lets you struggle.

Trust the process. Have faith that the path is unfolding precisely as it should, even when it looks nothing like you expected.

STEP 4: **Maintain a Positive State Regardless of What Manifests**

Everything that happens serves a purpose—even if you can't see it immediately.

So-called "negative" events are often:

• Redirections guiding you away from what wouldn't serve you
• Course corrections aligning you with something better
• Opportunities for expansion and growth you didn't know you needed

Your state of being determines what you attract next. By maintaining a positive state—not forced positivity, but genuine trust and openness—you ensure that even obstacles become stepping stones.

When you stay aligned, setbacks transform into setups. Delays become divine timing. Closed doors reveal open windows.

STEP 5: **Recognize That Synchronicity Is the Organizing Principle of Reality**

When you follow your excitement, the universe coordinates events to support you.

People show up at the perfect moment. Resources appear when you need them. Opportunities align in ways that defy logic.

This is not luck. This is not coincidence. **This is divine order —the natural outcome of alignment.**

Synchronicity is the universe's way of confirming: *"Yes. You're on the path. Keep going."*

A NOTE **on Practical Application**

Following your excitement doesn't mean abandoning your responsibilities or making reckless decisions. It means finding what excites you most **within your current reality**. If you have to go to work to pay your bills, the excitement isn't "skip work and go to the beach"—that's escapism, not alignment. The excitement might be: "How can I bring more presence to this work? What's the most fulfilling way to approach my responsibilities? What excites me during my break, or after work?" Excitement operates within the life you're living, not by destroying it. As you consistently follow this thread—choosing the most exciting available option in each moment —you'll find your reality gradually shifting to support more of what truly lights you up. It's a practice. Start where you are.

WHY THE FORMULA WORKS: **The Physics of Alignment**

The Formula works because it harmonizes you with the fundamental structure of existence itself.

When you act on excitement, you are:

✓ **Connecting to your Higher Mind's guidance system** – You're tapping into intelligence beyond your limited physical perspective

✓ **Aligning with your soul's purpose and path** – You're moving in the direction you came here to move

✓ **Operating from your natural frequency** – You're broadcasting a signal that attracts harmonious experiences

✓ **Becoming a co-creator with the universe** – Rather than forcing, controlling, or resisting, you're flowing with the current of reality itself

. . .

THIS ISN'T METAPHOR. **This is mechanics.**

When you align your frequency with excitement, you literally tune into the version of reality where that path unfolds. The Fourth Law—reality mirrors consciousness—activates. The universe reflects back what you're emanating.

THE COMPLETE SYSTEM: **How Excitement Contains Everything You Need**

When you consistently follow The Formula, something remarkable happens: **Your excitement reveals itself as a complete guidance system containing every tool necessary for your expansion.**

Life stops being a struggle. It becomes a flow. Reality shifts from something you fight against to something you dance with.

Here's what your excitement actually provides:

THE FUEL **for your journey** - It generates the motivation, energy, and clarity to take the next step. You're never pushing yourself; you're being pulled forward by genuine desire.

THE ORGANIZING INTELLIGENCE - It arranges experiences in the optimal sequence. What needs to happen first happens first. People, resources, and opportunities show up in perfect timing—not your timing, but divine timing.

THE NATURAL CURRENT - It shows you the path of least resistance. You're not forcing doors open; you're walking through the ones already opening. Effort becomes ease.

. . .

THE CONNECTING **thread** - It links seemingly random experiences into a cohesive journey. Looking back, you see how each "unrelated" event was actually building toward something larger. Nothing was wasted.

THE FEEDBACK MECHANISM - It reveals your limiting beliefs by showing you where the excitement stops or turns to resistance. When you hit a block, it's not failure—it's information. Something within you needs to shift, and your excitement just showed you exactly what.

WHAT ACTUALLY HAPPENS **When You Live This Way**

When you practice The Formula consistently, tangible transformations emerge:

Resistance dissolves. Life becomes effortless—not because everything is easy, but because you're no longer swimming upstream. You're moving with the current of your own natural energy.

Synchronicities multiply dramatically. What once seemed rare becomes your norm. You consistently find yourself in the right place, at the right time, with the right people—not through control or manipulation, but through alignment.

Abundance flows naturally in all forms. Money, opportunities, relationships, resources—all align. You discover that abundance isn't something you chase; it's something that follows alignment.

Relationships become more harmonious and supportive. You attract people who resonate with your true frequency. Toxic connections naturally fall away. Nourishing ones appear.

Your purpose clarifies through lived experience. You don't need to figure it out mentally—it reveals itself through action. Each excited step leads to the next, and the path unfolds.

Fear and anxiety fade as trust deepens. You stop worrying about the "how" and surrender to the unfolding. You've seen the system work enough times that trust becomes natural.

When you practice The Formula, your reality transforms to harmonize with the version of yourself that is completely synchronized with joy, passion, and abundance.

The universe moves with you. And reality becomes effortless.

LIVING in Alignment with Universal Laws

The Formula is not a belief system—**it is a structural mechanism of how reality operates.**

Remember the Five Laws:

• **First Law:** You exist. You always will.

• **Second Law:** The One is the All, and the All is the One. Everything is connected.

• **Third Law:** Everything is here and now. All possibilities exist in the present moment.

• **Fourth Law:** What you put out is what you get back. Reality mirrors consciousness.

• **Fifth Law:** Everything changes—except these fundamental laws.

The Formula is how you align with these laws in practical, moment-to-moment living.

Following The Formula is the key to unlocking a life of effortless manifestation, fulfillment, and alignment with your highest self. This is not wishful thinking—it is the fundamental physics of existence.

CHAPTER 14 KEY Takeaways

• The Formula is the simplest yet most powerful approach to living your best life

• Act on your highest excitement with integrity and without attachment to outcome

• Excitement operates within your current reality—not by abandoning responsibilities

• This creates a positive chain reaction that elevates every aspect of your existence

• Even if you understood nothing else in this book, practicing The Formula would transform your life

• Following your excitement is following divine guidance in its purest form

• Synchronicity is the organizing principle of reality—trust it

• Consistency is key—this is a practice, not a one-time event

• Your state of being determines what you attract next

• The Formula works because it aligns you with the fundamental structure of existence itself

FIFTEEN

CHAPTER 15: ENHANCED SPIRITUAL GLOSSARY: RECLAIMING DIVINE KNOWING

Divine Knowing: Spiritual Terminology Reference

A NOTE **to the Reader**

The following spiritual terminology represents my current understanding and interpretation of these concepts as they align with my spiritual journey and Divine Knowing. These definitions may differ from traditional religious or academic interpretations, as they reflect the evolved understanding that comes from direct spiritual experience and study of multiple wisdom traditions.

I encourage you to refer to this glossary as you progress through the book whenever you encounter terms that may be unfamiliar or when you wish to deepen your understanding of the spiritual concepts presented. Remember, these are not absolute definitions but rather invitations to explore these concepts through your own spiritual lens and experience.

Use this as a reference tool to enhance your journey through Divine Knowing, allowing these definitions to serve as stepping stones toward your own direct spiritual understanding.

. . .

A NOTE **on Independent Study and Personal Discernment**

The spiritual teachers, channeled entities, and wisdom traditions referenced throughout this book represent decades of profound teachings—far more than any single volume could contain. While I have shared the aspects that most deeply resonate with my journey and understanding of Divine Knowing, each of these sources offers vast depths of wisdom waiting to be explored.

I strongly encourage you to do your own independent study. Don't simply accept my interpretations or selections. Go directly to the source materials. Listen to Bashar's transmissions. Read Neville Goddard's lectures. Explore Eckhart Tolle's teachings. Study Abraham-Hicks. Investigate the mystical traditions I've referenced. Watch, read, listen, and most importantly—discern for yourself.

Your journey of Divine Knowing is uniquely yours. What resonates deeply with me may not resonate with you, and what I've overlooked might be exactly what your soul needs to hear. Use your own divine knowing as your ultimate guide.

As you explore these teachings:

• Notice what creates expansion and resonance within you

• Pay attention to what brings clarity rather than confusion

• Trust your internal compass more than any external authority—including mine

• Take what serves your growth and leave the rest without judgment

• Remember that spiritual truth reveals itself through direct experience, not just intellectual understanding

Each teacher, each channeled entity, each wisdom tradition offers a unique facet of the infinite diamond of truth. By exploring widely and discerning deeply, you build your own direct relationship with divine intelligence—which is, ultimately, the entire point of this book.

Your divine knowing will guide you to exactly what you need, when you need it. Trust that process. And enjoy the journey of discovery.

A NOTE **on Divine Terminology**

Throughout this book, you will encounter many different terms for the Divine Source of all existence. I intentionally utilize an ever-broadening list of references including: God, All That Is, Source, Source of All Light, Divine Father, Divine Mother, Divine Creator, The One, Universal Intelligence, and others. This variety serves a specific spiritual purpose.

The term "God" has been burdened with negative connotations and limiting interpretations over the centuries through religious control and misunderstanding. In an attempt to provide fresh insight and bypass conditioned responses, I employ diverse terminology to help you connect with the pure essence behind the name. What matters is not the specific term used, but the knowing, understanding, and connection behind the usage of that name.

Each term offers a different facet of the infinite Divine—like viewing a diamond from various angles. Allow these different expressions to expand your perception and help you find the terminology that most deeply resonates with your own spiritual understanding and connection to the Source of all existence.

THE FIVE LAWS **OF THE UNIVERSE**

LAW 1: **Eternal Existence** - You exist. This affirms that your existence is not temporary, accidental, or insignificant. You are an eternal being, a permanent aspect of the infinite consciousness that is God. Your existence transcends physical form and continues beyond bodily death.

. . .

LAW 2: **Unity** - The All Is the One, and the One Is the All. Everything in existence is interconnected and part of the same divine consciousness. There is no true separation—only the illusion of separation that allows for individual experience and growth.

LAW 3: **Presence** - Everything Is Here and Now. The only reality is the present moment. Past and future are mental constructs. All power, peace, joy, love, and abundance exist in the eternal now, waiting to be recognized and experienced.

LAW 4: **Reflection (Reality Mirrors Consciousness)** - What You Put Out Is What You Get Back. The universe functions as an intelligent mirror, reflecting your internal states back to you in external reality. Your thoughts, emotions, beliefs, and actions shape the reality you experience.

LAW 5: **Change** - Everything Changes Except the Five Laws. Change is the only constant in the universe. Everything is in continuous transformation, yet these five immutable laws remain steadfast as the foundation of reality across all dimensions.

FOUNDATIONAL SPIRITUAL TERMS

DIVINE KNOWING - The direct recognition of one's eternal nature and divine inheritance. An inside understanding of how life works, more importantly how mastery in life works. It's the realization of what the experience of earth, this Master Class, is intended to teach and be used for.

HOLOGRAPHIC REALITY/UNIVERSE - The understanding that reality is an interconnected, multidimensional projection of consciousness where every part contains the whole. Each individual consciousness contains the blueprint of universal consciousness, explaining why personal transformation affects external reality.

VIBRATIONAL FREQUENCY - The unique energetic signature of every being, thought, emotion, and creation. Everything vibrates at specific frequencies, and like frequencies attract like frequencies. Your frequency is determined by your thoughts, emotions, beliefs, and consciousness.

ALIGNMENT - LIVING in conscious harmony with divine truth and your highest self. Being in energetic resonance with your authentic nature and divine purpose. Occurs when thoughts, emotions, actions, and beliefs harmonize with universal principles.

MANIFESTATION - The conscious creation of reality through focused intention, belief, and vibrational alignment. Not forcing things to happen, but allowing what exists in potential to become visible by shifting your resonant frequency to match your desires.

CHANNELING/CHANNELED **Information** - The process of receiving and transmitting information, wisdom, or energy from non-physical sources, higher consciousness, or spiritual guides. Includes teachings from ascended masters, collective consciousness, or higher-dimensional beings.

SYNCHRONICITY - MEANINGFUL COINCIDENCES that occur when you are in alignment with divine flow. Events, people, and opportunities appearing at perfect timing to support spiritual growth and life purpose, demonstrating the interconnected nature of existence.

METAPHYSICAL - RELATING to the nature of reality beyond the physical world. Concerning fundamental principles that govern existence, consciousness, and the relationship between mind, spirit, and matter.

REDEFINED TRADITIONAL TERMS

GOD - TRADITIONAL: A separate being ruling over creation. Divine Knowing: The Source of all things, including you. The infinite intelligence that you are one with. The creative force expressing itself through all existence.

CHRIST/CHRIST **Consciousness** - Traditional: A title for Jesus, the Son of God. Divine Knowing: The embodied divine consciousness, awakened in all beings. The awareness of oneness with all that is. The state of fully realized divine potential.

KINGDOM OF GOD - TRADITIONAL: A place in the afterlife. Divine Knowing: A state of divine knowing within each human—the awareness of your oneness with God. A dimension of consciousness accessible here and now.

HOLY SPIRIT - TRADITIONAL: God's spiritual presence. Divine Knowing: The divine intelligence flowing through all life, guiding and illuminating. The active principle of divine consciousness within creation.

GRACE - TRADITIONAL: God's unmerited favor. Divine Knowing: The effortless flow of divine energy aligning all things perfectly. The natural state of divine support that flows when you are in alignment.

REPENTANCE - TRADITIONAL: Feeling sorrow for sins and changing behavior. Divine Knowing: A shift in consciousness, returning to divine awareness. A change of mind that aligns you with higher truth.

HEAVEN - TRADITIONAL: A perfect place where God resides. Divine Knowing: A dimension of consciousness aligned with divine love, unity, peace, and joy. A state of being accessible in the present moment.

HELL - TRADITIONAL: A place of eternal suffering for the wicked. Divine Knowing: A state of separation from divine awareness, a self-imposed illusion. The experience of being disconnected from your true nature.

. . .

MIRACLE - TRADITIONAL: An event that defies natural laws. Divine Knowing: A realization of divine truth beyond physical limitations. The natural result of operating from higher spiritual laws.

FAITH - TRADITIONAL: The substance of things hoped for The evidence of things not seen. Divine Knowing: The unwavering certainty in divine knowing that creates transformation. Knowing rather than believing.

LIGHT - TRADITIONAL: A metaphor for goodness and purity. Divine Knowing: The energy of divine awareness and creation. The fundamental force that illuminates consciousness.

DARKNESS - TRADITIONAL: A metaphor for evil and sin. Divine Knowing: The absence of divine knowing, an illusion that dissolves in truth. Not evil, but simply lack of awareness.

DIVINE WILL - TRADITIONAL: God's predetermined plan. Divine Knowing: Your ability to create your highest reality in alignment with divine flow. The harmony between personal will and universal intelligence.

JUDGMENT - TRADITIONAL: God's final verdict on humanity. Divine Knowing: The reflection of your own consciousness upon yourself. The natural consequence of the Law of Reflection.

ETERNAL LIFE - TRADITIONAL: Living forever in heaven.

Divine Knowing: Realizing your eternal nature beyond physical existence. Recognition that you are an immortal spiritual being.

LOVE - TRADITIONAL: A deep emotion or affection. Divine Knowing: The fundamental force of divine energy sustaining all things. The creative power that binds all existence together.

TRUTH - TRADITIONAL: Something factual and provable. Divine Knowing: The highest vibration of knowing, beyond perception. Direct spiritual knowing that transcends mental understanding.

WISDOM - TRADITIONAL: Knowledge and discernment. Divine Knowing: The ability to see through illusion and into divine clarity. Spiritual insight that guides right action.

POWER - TRADITIONAL: Control or authority over something. Divine Knowing: The force of divine creation within you, shaping reality. Your inherent ability to create and transform.

SACRIFICE - TRADITIONAL: Giving up something valuable for a higher purpose. Divine Knowing: An act of realignment with divine truth, releasing attachments. Letting go of what no longer serves your highest good.

REDEMPTION - TRADITIONAL: Deliverance from sin through Jesus' sacrifice. Divine Knowing: The return to self-realization, stepping out of illusion. Remembering your true divine nature.

. . .

GLORY - TRADITIONAL: Great honor or praise given to God. Divine Knowing: The radiance of divine presence within all beings. The natural expression of awakened consciousness.

PEACE - TRADITIONAL: A state of tranquility and absence of conflict. Divine Knowing: The state of knowing that all things are in divine harmony. Inner stillness that comes from spiritual alignment.

SPIRITUAL PRACTICE TERMS

AAA FORMULA - ACKNOWLEDGE, Appreciate, Allow - A spiritual framework for welcoming divine abundance. Acknowledge what is present, appreciate its value, and allow the natural flow of divine provision.

ALIGNMENT AND FLOW - The state of being in harmony with divine will and natural universal rhythms. When thoughts, emotions, and actions are synchronized with your highest truth and purpose.

ASCENSION - The conscious process of ascending into higher states of divine awareness by releasing resistance to our true nature. Spiritual evolution toward greater consciousness and divine realization.

AWAKENING - The realization of one's infinite existence and divine nature. The process of remembering who you truly are beyond physical identity and limitations.

. . .

DECLARATION - THE PRACTICE of speaking with divine authority to shape reality. Conscious use of the creative power of words aligned with divine truth.

ENERGY FREQUENCY - The measurable output of one's spiritual frequency and alignment. The vibrational signature that determines what you attract and experience.

FAITH ACTIVATION - The intentional activation of faith through knowing and speaking divine truth. Moving from hope to certainty through spiritual practice.

MASTER CLASS - EARTH as a sacred school where souls refine their mastery of divine power. The understanding that life experiences are opportunities for spiritual growth and mastery.

ONENESS - The lived experience of absolute unity with the Source. The recognition that all existence is interconnected and expressions of the same divine consciousness.

QUANTUM PRAYER - A prayer that operates from divine knowing, rather than requesting from lack. Prayer that acknowledges what already is rather than begging for what isn't.

REFLECTIVE MIRROR - REALITY as a mirror reflecting one's inner state, guiding self-awareness. The principle that external experiences reflect internal consciousness.

. . .

SACRED GEOMETRY - The recognition that all forms and patterns in nature reflect divine intelligence. The mathematical principles that underlie creation and consciousness.

SECOND COMING - TRADITIONAL: JESUS' physical return to Earth. Divine Knowing: The mass awakening of humanity into divine knowing, of their oneness with all that is. The collective realization of Christ consciousness.

SPIRITUAL FREEDOM - FREEDOM of the soul. The freedom to choose your thoughts, reactions, point of attraction, and how you define circumstances in your reality in an empowering way.

THE FORMULA - BASHAR'S five-step practical framework for living in complete alignment with divine flow and the organizing principle of reality. The Formula bridges spiritual understanding and daily application, providing the precise mechanism for navigating life through your highest excitement. The five steps are: (1) Act on your highest passion, excitement, or curiosity—no matter how small; (2) Act on it to the best of your ability, taking it as far as you can go; (3) Take this action with absolutely zero insistence on what the outcome should be; (4) Maintain a positive state regardless of what manifests; (5) Recognize that synchronicity is the organizing principle of reality that coordinates perfect timing. Excitement is not random or frivolous—it is your Higher Mind's precise guidance system, a compass pointing toward your optimal path and highest alignment. The Formula demonstrates that your excitement functions as a complete system containing everything you need: the fuel for your journey, the organizing intelligence that arranges experiences optimally, the natural current showing the path of least resistance, the connecting thread linking experiences into coherent growth, and the feedback mechanism revealing limiting beliefs. When practiced consistently within your current reality (not by abandoning responsibilities but by finding excitement within your circumstances), The Formula creates sustainable transformation. Reality gradually shifts to support more of what lights you up, synchronicities multiply, abundance flows naturally, and life becomes effortless—not because everything is easy, but because you're flowing with the current of your own natural energy rather than swimming upstream. The Formula works because it harmonizes you with the fundamental structure of existence itself, activating the Five Laws in your direct experience and demonstrating that manifestation is not a technique but the natural result of alignment.

CONSCIOUSNESS AND REALITY **TERMS**

OMNISCIENCE - TRADITIONAL: God's ability to know all things. Divine Knowing: The ability to access infinite wisdom through divine connection. The potential for unlimited knowing through spiritual alignment.

OMNIPOTENCE - TRADITIONAL: God's unlimited power. Divine Knowing: The internal realization of limitless creative force within. Recognition of your divine creative power.

OMNIPRESENCE - TRADITIONAL: God's presence everywhere at once. Divine Knowing: The understanding that divine presence permeates all existence, including oneself. Recognition that you are never separate from divine consciousness.

. . .

MANIFESTATION FIELD - The conscious manifestation of divine reality through focused thought and vibration. The energetic space where intention meets creation.

PARALLEL REALITIES - The understanding that multiple versions of reality exist simultaneously, and we shift between them based on our vibrational frequency and consciousness.

QUANTUM FIELD - The underlying field of infinite potential from which all reality emerges. The space of pure possibility that responds to consciousness and intention.

HIGHER SELF - The aspect of your consciousness that exists beyond physical limitations and maintains connection to divine wisdom and your soul's purpose.

SOUL CONTRACT - PRE-BIRTH agreements made at the soul level regarding the experiences, relationships, and lessons chosen for spiritual growth in this lifetime.

UNIVERSAL PRINCIPLES

Law of Attraction - The principle that like attracts like in terms of vibrational frequency. What you focus on with emotion and belief is drawn into your experience.

Law of Reflection - The principle that external reality reflects internal consciousness. Your outer world mirrors your inner state of being.

Law of Vibration - Everything in existence vibrates at

specific frequencies. Changing your vibration changes what you attract and experience.

Law of Resonance - The principle that you naturally attract and align with energies, people, and experiences that match your dominant frequency. Your energetic signature acts as a tuning fork, drawing into your reality whatever resonates at the same vibrational level.

"REMEMBER, *these definitions are invitations to explore and experience these concepts for yourself. True spiritual understanding comes not from intellectual knowledge alone, but from direct experience and inner knowing. Allow these terms to serve as doorways to your own divine realization.*"

SPIRITUAL REFERENCES LEXICON

TEACHERS, **Entities, and Cultural Context**

A Note on References: The following lexicon provides context for the spiritual teachers, channeled entities, biblical references, and cultural concepts mentioned throughout this book. These explanations are offered to enhance understanding while maintaining the high vibrational essence of these wisdom sources. Each reference represents a facet of the infinite ways divine truth expresses itself through various messengers and teachings.

CHANNELED ENTITIES

ABRAHAM

A collective consciousness channeled through Esther Hicks for over 40 years, providing profound teachings on the Law of Attraction, alignment, and joyful living. Their consistent message of following your highest excitement and maintaining vibrational alignment perfectly complements Divine Knowing principles. Like Bashar, Abraham represents access to higher-dimensional wisdom through the channeling process.

Website: https://www.abraham-hicks.com/

Additional platform: https://www.abrahamnow.com/

BASHAR

A channeled entity speaking through Darryl Anka for over 40 years, offering consistent, high-quality spiritual information. As a technical support engineer with 20-30 years of experience solving complex issues, I understand escalation to developers who have deeper access to the code base. Channeling operates similarly—these entities have access to higher-dimensional understanding. Most notably in this book, Bashar's teachings include both the Five Laws of the Universe—the fundamental principles that govern all reality—and The Formula, a five-step process for living in alignment with divine flow through following your highest excitement. The Formula provides a practical mechanism for applying the Five Laws in daily life, demonstrating that excitement is not random but rather your Higher Mind's precise guidance system directing you toward your highest alignment. Together, these teachings form a complete framework: the Five Laws explain how reality operates, while The Formula shows you how to navigate reality in alignment with those laws. Channeling is the process by which an individual consciously connects with and communicates messages from non-physical beings, higher consciousness, or divine intelligence. This is identical to what happens in traditional black churches when a preacher says, "Lord, I now surrender my vessel to you. Use my body, speak through me. Let these words not be my words, let they be your words. Let my thoughts be your thoughts, let my will be your will." It's the same spiritual process, just outside the church framework. When a pastor effectively surrenders, they can know nothing about your life yet preach a sermon that speaks directly to your situation.

Website: https://www.bashar.org/

THEO

THEO is described as a collective of twelve archangelic beings communicating through a human channel (Sheila Gillette) via a process called Soul Integration™. Their focus is on guiding individuals into a state of "masterfulness," supporting spiritual and psychic expansion, and facilitating the emergence of one's own divine knowing. While less traditional in format than many other teachers listed, THEO offers a distinctive path for those interested in channeled spiritual guidance and conscious evolution.

Website: https://asktheo.com/

Note: The nature of THEO's teaching is metaphysical and channelled rather than traditional, which may influence how one engages with it.

DOLORES CANNON - HYPNOTHERAPIST, **Past Life Regressionist**

Dolores Cannon was a pioneering hypnotherapist and past life regressionist who developed the Quantum Healing Hypnosis Technique (QHHT). Through her deep trance hypnotherapy sessions, she accessed profound spiritual information that she compiled into numerous books. Her most notable works include The Convoluted Universe series, The Three Waves of Volunteers and the New Earth, and Between Death and Life. Her work explores themes of reincarnation, extraterrestrial contact, lost civilizations, and the nature of consciousness. Learn more and access her work at www.dolorescannon.com or find her books on major retailers.

. . .

NEALE DONALD WALSCH - AUTHOR, **Spiritual Messenger**

Neale Donald Walsch is a spiritual teacher and author best known for his groundbreaking Conversations with God series, which began in the mid-1990s. Through a process he describes as inspired writing or divine dialogue, Walsch has authored numerous books that explore humanity's relationship with the Divine, the nature of reality, and practical spiritual living. His most celebrated works include Conversations with God: Book 1, Friendship with God, and Home with God. His teachings offer profound insights into living an awakened, purposeful life. Visit www.nealedonaldwalsch.com or find his books wherever books are sold.

SPIRITUAL TEACHERS

ECKHART TOLLE

German-Canadian spiritual teacher and author best known for "The Power of Now" (1997) and "A New Earth" (2005). His teachings on presence, consciousness, and transcending ego-mind align perfectly with Divine Knowing principles. Tolle's emphasis on living in the present moment and recognizing the illusory nature of mental suffering provides practical pathways to spiritual awakening that complement the Five Laws of the Universe.

Website: https://eckharttolle.com/

NEVILLE **Goddard**

(1905-1972) Barbadian-American mystic and New Thought teacher who taught that imagination is the creative power of God within each person. His approach to biblical interpretation through mystical Christianity and his teachings on manifestation through imagination provide profound insights into the creative nature of consciousness that align with Divine Knowing principles of reality creation.

Website: https://www.neville-goddard.com/

Note: The site appears to be a curated archive of his work rather than a personally maintained site (he is deceased), so the "officiality" is assumed but not guaranteed.

KENNETH HAGIN

(1917-2003) American Pentecostal preacher and founder of the Word of Faith movement. Known for his teachings on faith, healing, and the believer's authority in Christ. His prayer frameworks, particularly the Ephesians 1:17-19 (KJV) prayer for wisdom and understanding, provided foundational spiritual practices that opened pathways to deeper divine understanding and direct spiritual connection.

Website: https://www.rhema.org/

CHARLES **Capps**

American minister and author in the Word of Faith movement, known for his teachings on the creative power of words and the authority of the believer. His insights into how spoken words carry creative power and how belief systems shape reality align with Divine Knowing principles about the vibrational nature of consciousness and manifestation.

REVEREND IKE

(1935-2009) Frederick J. Eikerenkoetter II, American minister known for his prosperity theology and positive-thinking teachings. His bold approach to spiritual abundance and self-empowerment challenged traditional religious limitations and provided early exposure to the concept that spirituality and material prosperity can coexist harmoniously.

JOSEPH MURPHY

(1898-1981) Irish-American author and New Thought minister, best known for "The Power of Your Subconscious Mind" (1963). Murphy's teachings on the creative power of the subconscious mind and how thoughts and beliefs shape reality directly align with Divine Knowing principles. His emphasis on using prayer, visualization, and positive affirmations to reprogram limiting beliefs and manifest desired outcomes provides practical tools that complement the understanding of consciousness as the creator of experience.

MARIANNE **Williamson**

American author, spiritual teacher, and political activist best known for her interpretations of "A Course in Miracles." Her book "A Return to Love" (1992) brought Course principles to mainstream audiences. Her teachings on love as the opposite of fear and her emphasis on spiritual transformation as the foundation for personal and social change align with Divine Knowing principles of consciousness evolution.

Website: https://mariannewilliamson.com/

MICHAEL BECKWITH

American New Thought minister, author, and founder of the Agape International Spiritual Center. Known for his teachings on spiritual evolution, consciousness expansion, and the four stages of spiritual unfoldment. Beckwith's emphasis on moving from victim consciousness to creator consciousness, and his understanding that we are spiritual beings having a human experience rather than human beings having a spiritual experience, directly aligns with

Divine Knowing principles. His work on cultivating a "beginner's mind" and his teachings on how spiritual practices can transform both individual and collective consciousness complement the Five Laws of the Universe and the understanding that reality is created from the inside out.

Website: https://www.agapelive.com/michael-beckwith

CULTURAL CONTEXTS

Atlanta Spiritual Events - References to spiritual networking and gathering culture, similar to traditional Sunday church services and Wednesday night bible study, but often in contemporary, non-denominational settings. These events represent the modern evolution of spiritual community gathering, where seekers come together to explore expanded consciousness and spiritual growth outside traditional religious frameworks.

SIXTEEN

CONCLUSION: YOUR JOURNEY INTO DIVINE KNOWING

Conclusion: The Choice to Remember

YOU HAVE NOW BEEN INTRODUCED to the fundamental principles that govern reality, consciousness, and your divine nature. But understand this: **This is not merely information—it is a transmission, a remembering of what you have always known at the deepest level of your being.**

Every word you've read, every concept explored, every law understood—these are not new teachings being added to you. They are ancient truths being *remembered* within you. You are not learning something foreign. You are recognizing something familiar.

You are not a human having a spiritual experience. You are a divine being having a human experience.

This is not philosophy. This is fact. This is the truth of your existence, whether you remember it or not.

Divine Knowing is not a destination to reach—it is a way of being to embody. It is the lived recognition that the Kingdom of God is within you. That you have direct access to infinite wisdom. That you are not separate from Source but are Source experiencing itself through your unique perspective.

Every moment—this moment, and the next, and the next—offers you a choice: Will you align with this truth, or will you forget it again?

The tools you have been given are not concepts to be studied and filed away. **The Five Laws, The Formula, the understanding of your mirror reality, the recognition of your inherent worthiness**—these are principles to be *lived*. They are keys that unlock the door. But you must turn them. You must walk through.

You are not here to follow anyone else's path. You are not here to wait for permission or validation. You are not here to prove your worthiness or earn your divinity.

You are here to remember your divine authority and to create from that place of knowing.

The greatest teachers throughout history—Jesus, Buddha, Krishna, the mystics and sages across all traditions—have all pointed to the same truth: **The power is within you. It always has been.**

They were not exceptional beings granted special access to God. They were beings who *remembered* their divine nature and lived from that remembrance. They demonstrated what becomes possible when a soul fully aligns with its truth.

And now they call you to do the same.

Not to worship them. Not to follow them. But to **become** what they demonstrated is possible.

This book is an invitation—not to believe something new, but to remember something ancient. An invitation to step into your power, to claim your birthright as a divine creator, and to live from the knowing that you are worthy, you are loved, and you are one with All That Is.

The question is not whether you are *capable* of living this truth. **You are.** You always have been. The capability is not in question.

The question is not whether you *deserve* this power. **You do.** Worthiness is not earned; it is inherent.

The question is not whether this is *real*. **It is.** Reality itself will prove it to you the moment you align with it.

The only question that remains is this:

Will you choose to remember?

Will you step into the divine knowing that you are an eternal being, inseparable from Source, capable of creating your reality through alignment with universal principles?

Will you practice The Formula? Will you trust your excitement? Will you maintain your positive state when reality tests your conviction?

Will you see the mirror of reality reflecting back your consciousness and use that feedback to refine your beliefs?

Will you recognize that every experience—every challenge, every synchronicity, every closed door and open window—is the universe conspiring to guide you back to remembrance?

Your journey into Divine Knowing begins with a single choice.

Not tomorrow. Not when you feel ready. Not when circumstances are perfect.

Now.

In this moment.

The choice to remember who you are.

Will you remember?

ABOUT THE AUTHOR

Michael Best is a spiritual teacher, engineer, and seeker who has spent over two decades studying and applying the principles of Divine Knowing. Raised in a traditional Baptist household in the South, his spiritual journey evolved through deep Biblical study, secular spirituality, and direct experience with channeled teachings from masters like Abraham and Bashar.

His transformation from religious tradition to divine empowerment was forged through real-life challenges—including his son's birth injury, marriage struggles, and financial hardships—where he learned to apply spiritual principles not as theory, but as practical tools for creating an empowered life.

Drawing from his engineering background, Michael brings a systematic, practical approach to spirituality that bridges the gap between ancient wisdom and modern understanding. His mission is to help others remember their divine nature and step into their full creative power without the limitations of religious dogma or spiritual dependency.

Michael lives with his wife Jamala and their children, continuing to apply and refine these principles daily. Divine Knowing represents over twenty years of spiritual study, personal transformation, and the practical application of universal laws that have completely transformed his life—and can transform yours.

www.ingramcontent.com/pod-product-compliance
Lightning Source LLC
Chambersburg PA
CBHW071214090426
42736CB00014B/2819